Teachers' Guide

Non-fiction Writing

SCAFFOLDS

Year 6

Written by
Mary Pattinson

HOPSCOTCH

EDUCATIONAL PUBLISHING

Published by
Hopscotch Educational Publishing Ltd,
29 Waterloo Place,
Leamington Spa CV32 5LA
Tel: 01926 744227

© 2002 Hopscotch Educational Publishing

Written by Mary Pattinson
Series design by Blade Communications
Cover illustration by Kirsty Wilson
Illustrated by Debbie Clark
Printed by Stephens and George

ISBN 1-904307-04-3

The author and publisher would like to express their grateful thanks to the staff and pupils of Norwich High School for Girls and the How Hill Trust.

Non-fiction writing
SCAFFOLDS

CONTENTS

Non-fiction writing scaffolds for Year 6

INTRODUCTION

Non-fiction Writing Scaffolds Year 6 is intended for use in schools to help teach children how to write effectively in a variety of non-fiction genres. It improves children's ability to organise their writing so that it has purpose by familiarising them with a system of planning which they can apply to any title. As they work through the units, the children assemble a portfolio of non-fiction texts containing genre-specific vocabulary and writing features. The chosen text types coincide with those in the Literacy Framework's text-level objectives.

Many non-fiction texts are essentially cross-curricular. Thus the ability to write specifically and purposefully about a subject will benefit other areas of study.

Each unit includes information and activities on at least one sentence-level objective. Therefore the book also enhances the children's knowledge of grammar, punctuation and style.

THE PROGRAMME CONTAINS:

a teachers' book comprising:

- notes for teachers on the genres
- a bibliography for each genre
- copies of exemplar texts together with teaching notes
- guidance on how to develop grammar and punctuation skills in children's writing
- guidance on how to write in the particular genre and on specific features of each non-fiction text.

a resource book of photocopiable material comprising:

- illustrated versions of the exemplar texts especially produced for children
- notes for the children on understanding the grammar and punctuation (optional reference material)
- photocopiable activity sheets to reinforce the grammar and punctuation (optional)
- notes and tips for the children on writing non-fiction texts (optional reference material)
- differentiated scaffolds which give the children choices and guide them through the course of the text they are about to write
- vocabulary banks for them to use and add to.

HOW TO USE THE PROGRAMME

1   After examining texts in the target genre, read and discuss the exemplar text with the children, using the notes in the margin to highlight the examples of the unit's teaching point and writing feature. The children should follow the text using their own illustrated version from the Resource book.

2   Next, read through and explain the 'Understanding the grammar and punctuation' section of the unit. The children can do the activities together, either orally or using whiteboards, or independently on paper.

3   Then explain the 'Helpful hints' and 'Writing features' sections of the unit to the children.

4   Read through the scaffolds with the children. Then give them the differentiated word banks and ask them to record their own vocabulary suggestions in the space provided.

5   Give the children time to plan, write and edit their non-fiction text. Each child can then store the best copies in a writing folder.

NOTES

When using the scaffolds, give the children strict time limits to plan and write each of the sections. This will give them practice in writing timed non-fiction texts as preparation for the Key Stage 2 writing test.

However, the system is entirely flexible. The activities in each unit, from reading the exemplar to composing their own text using the scaffolds, can be used in shared or guided time, with the children working collaboratively or individually.

The sequential order of activities for each unit coincides exactly with the sequence for the teaching of writing outlined in Grammar for Writing (DfEE 0107/200). First the model can be discussed and its grammatical and thematic features interrogated during shared reading. Next the grammar and punctuation activities can be undertaken to reinforce the children's understanding of the relevant sentence-level objectives. The helpful hints section, scaffolds, and vocabulary banks support the teacher and children in shared writing sessions and in subsequent guided and independent writing.

The method works well with children of all abilities and with bilingual pupils, as it offers the security of a detailed framework and a bank of appropriate vocabulary together with the challenge of a grammar and writing features component for each unit.

The units fulfil the text-level and sentence-level requirements of the NLS Framework for Year 6 and revise components from Year 5, many of which feature in the Key Stage 2 tests. The following units may be used specifically in literacy lessons or they may be linked with work in other curriculum areas and used accordingly.

UNIT 1
Genre: autobiographies (T1, T12, T13)
Grammar and punctuation: imagery – similes, metaphors, personification, clichés, sensory images; parentheses; dashes. (T1, S6)
Writing features: the narrator as the subject; influences on the writer; descriptive writing; bias.

UNIT 2
Genre: biography (T1, T11, T14)
Grammar and punctuation: taking notes (T3, T17, T18); first and third person; capital letters.
Writing features: writing chronologically – the opening, childhood to adulthood, young adulthood/maturity.

UNIT 3
Genre: informal letters
Grammar and punctuation: using slang (T3, S2, T2, T20); apostrophes for omission and for possession.
Writing features: layout, structure and audience.

UNIT 4
Genre: formal letters – to complain, to inform, to persuade (T2, T20)
Grammar and punctuation: formal language (T2, S2); simple, compound and complex sentences; using commas (T2, S3).
Writing features: format, style and tone.

UNIT 5
Genre: instructions (T3, S1)
Grammar and punctuation: verbs and verb tenses (T3, T16); the use of the imperative (T2, S2); layout punctuation.
Writing features: organisation methods – numbered points and bullets, subheadings with paragraphs, continuous writing.

UNIT 6
Genre: leaflets and advertisements (T1, T12, T3, S1)
Grammar and punctuation: alliteration; puns; punctuating statements, questions, commands and exclamations.
Writing features: persuasive devices (T3, S1); language, fact and opinion (T1, T11); illustrations.

UNIT 7
Genre: recounts and chronological reports (T3, S1)
Grammar and punctuation: adjectives; adverbs; using capital letters for emphasis; asterisks.
Writing features: style and structure – personal and impersonal writing (T2, S2, T3, T20); orientation and reorientation; sentence starters.

UNIT 8
Genre: non-chronological texts – reports and explanations (T1, T12, T17, T3, S1, T15, T20)
Grammar and punctuation: paragraphs and linking paragraphs (T3, T21); the use of the passive voice; colons and semicolons (T2, S1, S6).
Writing features: gathering information and acknowledging sources including using quotes and writing a bibliography.

UNIT 9
Genre: journalistic writing (T1, T15, T16, T18)
Grammar and punctuation: clauses; phrases (T2, S3); prepositions; quotation marks.
Writing features: balance and bias; headlines (T3, S2); the inverted pyramid.

UNIT 10
Genre: discursive texts (T2, T15, T16, T18, T19)
Grammar and punctuation: using connectives (T1, S4, S5); how punctuation can alter meaning.
Writing features: structuring arguments.

Autobiographies

The word 'autobiography' is made up of three Greek words:

autos – self
bios – life
graphein – to write

In an autobiography, the writer is the main character because he is writing about himself. It is a personal story in which the writer selects episodes and events from his life that he thinks will interest the reader.

The writer has to be selective because it is impossible to remember every detail of his life, so he picks out relevant elements to inform and interest his reader. The views he expresses in his autobiography are obviously biased. He may give much more emphasis to some aspects of his life whilst others are not mentioned. In fact he can choose and use just what he wishes his audience to know. In this way, the writer can stress a particular viewpoint, whether it is a view of an event or an issue in recent history or a political view.

When reading an autobiography, it is interesting to think about why the author has written his story, who his audience is and what message he may be trying to put across. The reader should also try to separate fact from opinion.

An autobiography differs from a biography in that the writer is able to include facts known only to him. He can describe his thoughts, feelings, opinions, values and goals, whereas a biographer can only describe what he thinks his subject feels. An autobiography also often includes much more detail about events since the writer has actually experienced these moments and does not have to rely upon second-hand knowledge.

An autobiography is always a first person account because the author is the subject of the narrative.

Note: The story is adapted from an autobiography written by Sophie Pattinson, aged 14.

Autobiographies

Examples of autobiographies

Boy by Roald Dahl (New Windmills, Heinemann)
Coming to England by Floella Benjamin (Puffin)
Out of India by Jamila Gavin (Pavilion Books)
War Boy by Michael Foreman (Puffin)
Zlata's Diary by Zlata Filipovic (Puffin)

Also
Poems by Michael Rosen and Jackie Kaye

(For advanced readers)
Chinese Cinderella by Adeline Yen Mah (Puffin)
Going Solo by Roald Dahl (New Windmills, Heinemann)

The children's illustrated version of this autobiography is on page 6 of the Resource book.

On arrival in an alien land[1]

(an extract from 'A different kind of Christmas')

<u>He wasn't there.</u>[2]

<u>Why not? Where was he?</u>[3]

Travel weary, dishevelled, excited and eagerly anticipating the reunion with Tom, my big brother, I had planned this moment for months, travelled over 5,000 miles and now here I was, baggage collected, through customs and <u>keenly scanning</u>[4] the sea of oriental faces for his blond head and his familiar grin.

But … no Tom.

I could feel anxiety flutter in my stomach <u>like the wings of a butterfly</u>[5] and panic rise like bile in my throat as my eyes darted up and down the arrivals lounge.

Where was he? Who to ask? Where to go? What to do?[3]

Everything was <u>alien</u>[6] – the people, the language, even the signs were written in unrecognisable Chinese characters. I was here, in China, 14 years old, on my own, and not a clue as to what to do next. What should have been the best day of my life was rapidly becoming a nightmare.

<u>Minutes ticked by, hours maybe…</u>[7]

"There you are!" A breathless and apologetic voice behind me, then I found myself enveloped in a giant bear hug.

"Sorry, Soph, I overslept. Come on, let's go!"

<u>Relief flooded through me; fear and disappointment were quickly forgotten and I could even find it quite amusing</u>[8] that I had travelled all these miles to see him and <u>he'd</u>[9] actually overslept on the big day of my arrival.

Tom grabbed my bag and guided me out into the freezing Beijing air.

"The taxi wouldn't wait; we'll catch a bus," said Tom and I was bundled on to an ancient ramshackle vehicle with black smoke belching from its exhaust. So much for luxurious travel!

That journey was most definitely hair-raising and one that <u>I'll</u>[9] never forget.

I'm told that <u>I tend to exaggerate and to jump to dramatic conclusions</u>[10] but I swear that I am not exaggerating when <u>I tell you</u>[11] that I saw my whole life flash before my eyes as the breath was literally knocked out of me. This bus looked like an ordinary bus but there the similarity ended. At each and every stop, more and more people clambered over each other to squeeze in, until it seemed that <u>at least two hundred people</u>[12] were crushed together! The noise! The air was fetid, thick with the strong tobacco smoke prevalent in China. <u>An occasional harsh clearing of the throat could be heard as someone hawked and spat a glob out of the window regardless of the unsuspecting pedestrians below.</u>[13]

1	The title introduces the subject of the autobiography – the feeling of being in a totally alien situation.
2	Short opening sentence to give impact and invite the reader to read on.
3	Questions – who, what, where, why? Indicates anxious state of mind.
4	Gives emphasis to anticipation rather than simply 'looked for'.
5	Simile to express anxiety.
6	Again, the use of the word 'alien' to help convey the feeling of helplessness.
7	In an overanxious state minutes seem like hours. Also, the use of the agentless passive creates tension.
8	Many different emotions reflecting state of turmoil.
9	The use of the shortened form gives an informal tone to the writing.
10	Gives a clue to the writer's personality. There is evidence of exaggeration throughout the passage. The reader needs to bear this in mind.
11	The use of the 2nd person gives the feeling of talking directly to and involving the reader.
12	Exaggeration.
13	References to cultural behaviour.

The bus grumbled[14] and wove its way along the main streets of Beijing; really wide streets but lacking any apparent system – no lanes as such – drivers simply criss-crossed at breakneck speed.

"It takes a lot of skill to drive in Beijing," remarked Tom dryly, observing the look of disbelief on my face.

"Yeah, sure," I said sarcastically, peeping out from behind my fingers.

"You need to know how to accelerate, brake and keep your hand permanently on the horn!" he joked.[15]

I ventured a look out of the window, my nose pressed against the glass. The roads were jam-packed with buses, taxis and bicycles. The din of car horns hooting, of people shouting and of bicycle bells incessantly ringing. Bicycles were everywhere – hundreds, no thousands of them! Men on bicycles, women and children on bicycles, bicycles[16] piled as high as houses[17] with crates of produce – bread, beer, fruit and even live chickens, all clucking and squawking and adding to the cacophony.

No vivid colours in this city, however. Drab grey skies matched drab grey buildings and even the people looked colourless and careworn – not a true reflection of their character, though, as I later came to discover[18], for the Chinese people are friendly, generous and eager to please.

We passed sights seen only before on television screens or in those geography picture books at school; the giant portrait of Chairman Mao looking stern-faced over Tiananmen Square, the vast grey, concrete ocean[19] of the square itself with Mao's mausoleum at its centre and the snaking[19] queues of people paying homage. Tom told me that whenever he comes to Tiananmen Square he watches, fascinated, as the people entering the tomb buy flowers to lay before the leader's embalmed body. Those very same flowers, however, are soon taken out again by officials, via a back route, and resold to the next unsuspecting bunch of visitors.[20] I found this hilarious and said I didn't believe a single word of his story!

As the bus rounded the square, glimpses flashed past us of young men and women going about their business, of old men in Mao suits sitting on benches, smoking and chatting, of soldiers, of policemen, of tourists.[21] And all around us was the dipping and soaring of giant decorative kites – kite-flying in Tiananmen Square being a traditional and popular pastime. It all seemed unreal, somehow, and I almost had to pinch myself to believe that I was actually there.

We rumbled on, passing shops and offices and huge apartment blocks until eventually our journey reached its end and, after a good deal of shoving and jostling, we managed to alight from the bus very near the university campus where Tom was studying.[22]

From the kerbs, street vendors were shouting and advertising their wares; buyers and sellers were bargaining over goods, prices were being knocked down and money was being exchanged. We were on the edge of one of Beijing's numerous street markets.

Tom hurried me through the rows of stalls intent on reaching the university and settling me in my room, but I was fascinated by the goods on offer and all the tempting bargains.

14 Personification.

15 A clue to Tom's personality and the fact that he feels much more relaxed and at home in the situation.

16 Repetition of the word 'bicycles' gives emphasis to sheer numbers.

17 Simile.

18 Hints that the writer, in the future, gets to know the people quite well and so probably does not remain a simple tourist.

19 Metaphors.

20 Use of an amusing anecdote to give extra information.

21 Less detail in description here since the bus is moving and only glimpses of life are captured.

22 First indication of what Tom is doing in China – obviously not a tourist but is used to living in the city.

Silks of every colour hung from high poles; clothes, cushions, bags – an array of red, gold, jade and vivid blue. Designer clothes at undreamed of prices hung alongside stalls with Rolex watches, leather goods and wonderful jewellery.

"All fake, of course," said Tom, "but who's to tell the difference?"[23]

And I stopped, time and time again, to admire and touch and wonder. Constantly we were badgered to buy, the vendors presuming us to be wealthy western tourists but Tom, in fluent Chinese, chatted and joked with them[24] whilst I mentally shopped for England!

The chance to shop here, in this market, was definitely too good to miss and I can assure you[25] that, before my trip was over, I had become quite adept at bargaining!

Soon we reached the food stalls and here the acrid stench of traffic fumes mingled with the sickliness of incense and some rather exotic and mouthwatering aromas.[26] Nothing, though, had prepared me for the weird and wonderful foods on offer. Many were recognisable – noodles, rice, meats, fruits – but others were quite disgusting! Newly hatched chicks, strung out on sticks and barbequed; live scorpions taken from a pot, allowed to roam over the table for our amusement and then skewered and roasted over a fire![27] Eat these? I don't think so![28]

But then we saw food we both recognised.

"Pancakes!" cried Tom. "Are you hungry? Let's eat!"

Thus, my first taste of China.[29]

---

23 The author is fascinated by the treasures to be found in the market. Tom, on the other hand, is more blasé. Hence this rather cynical comment.

24 Reference to Tom's ability to communicate with the locals, hinting that this trip may not be simply devoted to visiting tourist attractions.

25 Appealing directly to the reader once again.

26 Descriptive writing using sensory images which help to bring writing to life. There are many others in the passage.

27 Unfamiliar foods quite daunting to western tastes.

28 Colloquial phrase – typical of the writer's age.

29 Pun on the word 'taste'. Literally tasting the food but also a first glimpse of the country.

Understanding the grammar and punctuation

Understanding the grammar and punctuation enables children to control the language they use and therefore to write more effectively.

Grammar pointers

Help the children to be aware of the following when writing their autobiographies.

Similes

A simile is an obvious comparison. When we use similes we are making a scene come alive by comparing our descriptions to something which the reader will immediately be able to visualise.

There are two common ways of making a comparison in speech and writing. We can use the link word 'like'

I could feel anxiety flutter in my stomach like the wings of a butterfly

Or we can use 'as ... as ...'

... bicycles piled as high as houses with crates of produce

Metaphors

A metaphor is a direct comparison between two things. Instead of saying a thing is like another, it says that a thing is another.

My feet were blocks of ice.

A metaphor enables us to create vivid images which make an experience more real to the reader. It is often stronger and more powerful than a simile and is also more difficult to recognise. A metaphor also refers to a word or phrase which does not have a literal meaning. Examples in the text are:

the vast ... ocean of the square

... snaking queues of people paying homage ...

Personification

Personification is a particular type of metaphor where an object is treated as if it were a living creature that can experience and feel emotion. For example:

... the bus grumbled ...

Clichés

A cliché is an expression that has been used too often and becomes so familiar that it has ceased to have much meaning. For example:

It's raining cats and dogs

Clichés should generally be avoided and similes and metaphors should be original and interesting.

Sensory images

A sensory image is an image that draws on one of the five senses (hearing, touch, smell, taste, sight). It is used to give the reader a sense of experiencing the same thing as the writer. For example:

the acrid stench of traffic fumes mingled with the sickliness of incense and some rather exotic ... aromas

Punctuation pointers

Parentheses

Brackets (parentheses) are used to enclose information which is additional to the main statement. The information enclosed in the brackets is called parenthesis and can be removed without changing the meaning of the sentence.

Parenthesis can take the form of a single word or a phrase. For example:

Beijing (Peking) is the capital city of China.
Beijing (also known as Peking) is the capital city of China.

It can also take the form of a date or even a complete sentence.

Understanding the grammar and punctuation

Dashes

Dashes may be found in pairs and these act in the same way as brackets or commas to enclose extra information. For example:

> *... wide streets but lacking any apparent system – no lanes as such – drivers simply criss-crossed at breakneck speed*

A single dash is often followed by an afterthought or conclusion to a sentence. For example:

> *... the people looked colourless and careworn – not a true reflection of their character.*

Dashes can also be used to emphasise a word or phrase. For example:

> *Bicycles were everywhere – hundreds, no thousands of them!*

The children's version of these notes is on page 10 of the Resource book.

Writing features

The narrator as the subject

An autobiography is always written in the first person, since the narrator is recounting events in his own life. Because he has experienced these events first-hand, he is able to describe in great detail his feelings, his reactions, his values and his goals so that we, as the reader, have a real sense of knowing the author. Certain phrases in Sophie's autobiography allow us glimpses of her personality. For example:

> *I could even find it quite amusing that I had travelled all these miles to see him and he'd actually overslept on the big day of my arrival.*

> *I tend to exaggerate and to jump to dramatic conclusions*

> *"Yeah, sure," I said sarcastically*

Influences on the writer

Explain to the children that in an autobiography, the author is able to describe the interaction between himself and other people. It may be a member of his family, as in the model, or it may be someone who has influenced him in some way and who has become an important person in his life. He is able to show clearly, through his writing, just how these people have made an impact on him.

Similarly, the author is able to recount events or describe places that have influenced his way of life or way of thinking. These events or places may not be significant in themselves. In fact they may simply be an account of a sports day or a day's outing; but because of something that has happened, such as 'unexpectedly winning that race' or 'the frightening experience of getting lost on an outing', it has become a memorable event and merits a detailed story.

Descriptive writing

Often the things that happen to us are best described by our feelings, for example Sophie feeling 'lost' in a foreign country:

> *I could feel anxiety flutter in my stomach like the wings of a butterfly*

Or her excitement at the vast array of goods on offer in the market:

> *I mentally shopped for England!*

Explain to the children that it is important to include vivid personal descriptions in order to involve the reader in the story.

Bias

Remind the children that when we are reading a first person account we are only being told what the author wants us to know and we are only seeing things from his point of view. Another person telling a story about the same event or place may well describe it with a totally different outlook. For example, when Sophie first sees things she could be expected to eat, she is horrified:

> *Newly hatched chicks, strung out on sticks and barbequed; live scorpions taken from a pot, allowed to roam over the table for our amusement and then skewered and roasted over a fire! Eat these? I don't think so!*

And yet for a Chinese person these 'delicacies' would be everyday fare.

There are helpful hints for children for writing an autobiography on page 13 of the Resource book.

Biographies

The word biography comes from the Greek words *bios* meaning 'life' and *graphein* meaning 'to write'. Biographies have been written for many hundreds of years and, in fact, one of the earliest biographers was Plutarch who wrote about the lives of famous Greeks and Romans.

A biography is an account of a person's life written by someone else, so, unlike an autobiography, it is usually written in the third person.

There are two kinds of biography – authorised and unauthorised.

An authorised biographer has the permission of the subject to write his life story and the biographer may even have been asked by the subject to write about him. Thus the writer will have a first-hand account of his subject's life and this type of work is usually considered to be more accurate than an unauthorised version.

An unauthorised biography is written without the subject's permission. The writer relies on information gained from sources such as books, letters, diaries and interviews with people who know the subject; thus the information is second-hand and may be less reliable.

The subject of a biography does not have to be famous, wealthy, powerful or an achiever, but rather someone who has made some kind of impact. He may be a living person, someone who has recently died or an historical figure.

The advantage of writing about people who are no longer living is that interviewees may talk more freely about them and so the account may be better balanced.

The biographer is telling a personal story of a character whom he may or may not know, but it is important to give a true picture of his life. He has to be selective because it is impossible to write about every detail of the subject's life, so he chooses relevant elements to inform and interest the reader. Unlike an autobiography, which gives a biased view of a person's life, the biography writer has access to a variety of sources of information and is thus able to give a more accurate and balanced picture.

A good biographer will bring the person alive for the reader and give them an insight into his personal accomplishments. Children enjoy reading biographies – they like learning about characters they can believe in, can identify with and can gain inspiration from.

Biographies

Examples of biographies

History
British History Makers series (Cherry Tree Books 1997)

Modern History
Heinemann Profiles series (Heinemann 1999)

Science and Technology
Groundbreakers series (Heinemann 2001)

Authors
Telling Tales (Mammoth)

The biography on page 14 is adapted from a story written by Sara ffrench-Constant when she was in Year 5. An illustrated version of this biography is featured on page 21 of the Resource book.

Ernest Henry Shackleton - a biography

Notes for a biography of Ernest Shackleton

Early Life
b. 15.2.1874 @ Kilkea Hse, Kildare, Ire. 9 bros & sis.
Father Henry, fmr m. Henrietta Gavan.[1]
Pot. crop fail – Dublin, f. to be Dr – move to London.
Sch. – at home – Dulwich Coll. – left @ 16 – Merch. Nvy[2]
m. Emily Dorman 1904 – ch. Raymond, Cecily, Edward.

1st Exp. 1901–3
N.A.E. with Scott (reached S.P. 1912) on Discovery – Antarctic – reached
400ml. from S.P.[2] – scurvy – home on Morning. Wanted to return.

2nd Exp. Nimrod 1907–9
1st as leader – New Zealand – towed to Ant. to save coal. Nimrod stuck in
ice. Shack., Adams, Wild, Marshall on foot – ran out of food – turn back –
97ml. from S.P. Put U.J. in ice.

3rd Exp. Endurance 1914–16
Most famous exp. 27 men 68 dogs. Endur. Named after motto.
Endur. stuck in ice 80ml. from S.P. Waited 10 mths. Endur. crushed by ice –
took 3 lifeboats – camped on ice floes.[3]
– 5 mths – thaw – sailed to Elephant Is. – uninhabited – 5 men to sea in 1
boat 800ml. – reach S. Georgia – wrong side.
Shack. and 2 men walk 17ml. & 36 hrs over mts. and glcs. to reach whaling
st. Strongness.
Later rescue men from Eleph. Is. All survived.

4th Exp. Quest 1921[4]
Set off. Sadly d. S. Georgia @ 47. (1922) bur. S. G.

....

Ernest Henry Shackleton

Quote
"For scientific leadership give me Scott; for swift and efficient travel give me
Amundsen. But when you are in a hopeless situation, when you are seeing no
way out, get down on your knees and pray for Shackleton."[5]

It was the most heroic bid for survival ever attempted. Three men wearing
wool suits, without tents or sleeping bags and with only a box of matches, an
axe and a rope, set out on an amazingly hazardous journey across uncharted
and inhospitable land, knowing that if they failed to reach safety, their own
lives and those of their fellow explorers would be lost.[6]

Shackleton's desperate journey across South Georgia came at the end of a
gruelling eighteen-month attempt to cross Antarctica.[7]

The Early Years

Ernest Henry Shackleton was born on the 15th February 1874 in Kilkea
House, County Kildare, Ireland. He had nine brothers and sisters and was the

---

1. Notes written in abbreviated form. Some are acknowledged abbreviations, such as:
   b. – born
   @ – at
   m. – married
   ml. – miles
   Is. – Island

2. Other abbreviations are invented by the writer, such as:
   S.P. – South Pole
   Merch. Nvy – Merchant Navy
   fmr – farmer

3. Key words are used as reminders of information gathered.

4. Underlined headings order facts in sequence.

5. Biography opens with a quote about the subject.

6. Opening paragraph written to capture the reader's imagination; makes him want to read on.

7. Adds more information and states what Shackleton is famous for.

second in the family. His father, Henry, was a farmer who married Henrietta Gavan in 1872. Soon after Ernest was born there was a terrible potato crop failure and life was made difficult for farmers, so when Ernest was six, his father left the farm, moved to Dublin and became a doctor.[8]

When Ernest was ten his family moved from Dublin to London. Until the age of eleven and a half he was taught at home by a governess but he later moved to Dulwich College as a day boy. His father wanted him to become a doctor but Ernest really wanted to become an explorer, so he left school at sixteen and joined the Merchant Navy.

In the summer of 1897 he met one of his sisters' friends, Emily Dorman, whom he married on 9th April 1904 at Christchurch, Westminster, London. They had three children whom they named Raymond, Cecily and Edward.

First Expedition   1901 –1903   The National Antarctic Expedition

Shackleton's first expedition was with Scott*[9] on the 'Discovery'. They left in the summer of 1901 for Antarctica. On the 30th December 1902 Scott, Shackleton and Wilson reached within 400 miles of the South Pole. This was the furthest south man had ever been.[10] Sadly, Shackleton became seriously ill with scurvy (a disease caused by lack of vitamin C in the diet) and had to return home on a relief ship called 'Morning'. He arrived back in England in 1903. He was, however, determined to return to Antarctica in the future, with his own expedition.

Second Expedition   1907 – 1909   The 'Nimrod' Expedition

Shackleton's second expedition was his first as party leader. He left London for New Zealand in 1907 on the 'Nimrod'. He then departed from New Zealand in 1908. The ship was towed to the Antarctic to save coal for the journey ahead.

The 'Nimrod' became stuck in ice so the party left the ship to travel over the ice. They even put a motor car on the ice; it was the first automobile on the ice.[11]

Shackleton, Adams, Wild and Marshall set out for the South Pole. Unfortunately, early in 1909 they ran out of food so they had to turn back. They got within 97 miles of the Pole, which was the furthest south anyone had reached. Shackleton planted in the ice the Union Jack that the Queen had given him.

Third Expedition   1914 – 1916   The 'Endurance' Expedition

This was Shackleton's most famous expedition.[12] On 1st August 1914 Shackleton, twenty-seven men and sixty-eight dogs sailed to Antarctica on the 'Endurance'; the ship was named after the family motto, 'By Endurance We Conquer' (Fortitudine Vincimus). The aim of the expedition was to cross Antarctica.

Things did not go as planned. Eighty miles short of the South Pole, the 'Endurance' stuck fast in ice. All the men could do was sit and wait until the ice melted and they could move once again. They whiled away the long hours and entertained themselves by playing football and hockey on the ice.

After ten months of being static, moving ice caused the 'Endurance' to be crushed and smashed, leaving the explorers no option but to abandon the ship, taking with them only three tiny lifeboats. The men pushed the lifeboats over the ice to safety and they pitched their tents for the night. From there, the next day, they watched the 'Endurance' sink beneath the icy seas.

8   This paragraph gives background information of the subject's family and birth. Subsequent paragraphs are written in chronological order and deal with the subject's life up to adulthood.

9   Footnote at the end of the biography tells briefly of Scott's achievement. The children may wish to make additional research on Scott.

10 Details achievement of first expedition.

11 The writer has included some details that she finds of particular interest.

12 After dealing with the first two expeditions quite briefly, the writer moves swiftly to the 'main event' of the biography ie what Shackleton is most famous for. This is made clear in the opening sentence of this section.

The group remained marooned on the ice floes for five months. Conditions were hazardous; killer whales smashed through the ice, ripping through it like tissue paper, and left gaping holes some 25 feet in diameter.[13] Then one night, the ice cracked and one of the men fell through. He was pulled out just in time![14]

The thaw had set in. So the next day the men put their boats in the water, pushed off and drifted towards the remote Elephant Island. Unfortunately, they found Elephant Island to be uninhabited so Shackleton knew he had to go on further to seek help.

Shackleton chose five of the fittest men and set off in one of the boats, a twenty foot open boat called 'James Caird,' on an 800 mile ocean voyage to seek help. They were navigating one of the most dangerous seas in the world. Fifteen days later, against all odds, they arrived at South Georgia but they soon discovered that they had landed on the wrong side of the island, the side where no one lived or visited. Shackleton and two of his men, Crean and Worsley decided to set off on foot to find the whaling station on the other side of South Georgia, a journey of 17 miles over mountains and glaciers – an achievement no one had ever before accomplished. The other three men, weak and ill, stayed behind.

The three explorers climbed over icy slopes and glaciers and reached a summit of 4,500 feet before descending once again. They ate and rested, but Shackleton was unwilling to sleep, for without tents or sleeping bags, the risk of freezing to death was very real. Eventually, after thirty-six hours, they spotted, in the distance, whaling boats and the small figures of whalers. They had reached the safety of Strongness whaling station.

Three and a half months later, after three unsuccessful attempts, Shackleton returned to Elephant Island to rescue the remaining 22 men who were still alive. They all made it safely back to England.

Fourth and final expedition   1921   The 'Quest' Expedition

Shackleton was desperate to go back to Antarctica so in 1921 he set out in the 'Quest'. Unfortunately on 5th January 1922 in South Georgia he suffered a heart attack and died at the age of 47. He was buried in South Georgia because his wife said "Bury him in South Georgia because that is where he wants to be."[15]

Quote
"You know, when you want an exclamation, don't say 'Great Scott!'
Say 'Great Shack!'"[16]

*Scott finally reached the South Pole in January 1912 but he was not the first because Amundsen reached it in December 1911.

Bibliography[17]
Alexander, Caroline. *The Endurance* (Knopf, 1998)
Herbert, Marie. *Great Polar Adventures* (Severn House, 1976)
Worsley, F. A. *Shackleton's Boat Journey* (Pimlico, 1940)
Children's Illustrated Encyclopedia (Dorling Kindersley, 1993)

Other Sources
'Encarta' 97
Internet – www.indigo.ie.
Film – 'Shackleton, Story of Survival' – BBC – Executive producer Michael Gunton

13 The writer uses imagery to give a vivid picture of the situation.

14 The account is factual but occasional mention of dramatic incidents adds interest for the reader giving an almost fictional appeal.

15 The final paragraph deals with the subject's death and burial.

16 Instead of a paragraph to sum up the story, the biographer uses this quote to reflect on the subject's life.

17 The writer records and acknowledges her sources of information.

Understanding the grammar and punctuation

Grammar pointers

Taking notes

Explain to the children that when they are researching a subject for a project, it is useful to be able to take notes quickly and efficiently. The purpose of note taking is to remind the writer of certain facts that he or she needs to include in his or her account without having to laboriously copy out details from the source material.

Notes are intended only for the person who is writing them; they should be as brief as possible but should be easily converted into information for others to read. The writer should be able to order his or her notes and expand on them in a logical manner.

When making notes from their research, the children may wish to use the following methods:

- Note the key words in sentences and paragraphs.
- Use headings to order facts in a logical sequence.
- Draw a web to organise facts.
- Use acknowledged and invented abbreviations.

First and third person

Ensure that the children can recognise the differences between writing in the first and the third person. Explain that the first person refers to the person who is speaking or writing. So an account written in the first person gives the impression of personal experience.

The third person refers to a third party, not the speaker or the person being spoken to. Writing in this way may reflect the opinions of a number of people.

An account written in the first person uses pronouns such as 'I', 'me', 'myself', 'mine', 'we', 'us', 'ourselves' and 'our' while a third person account will include pronouns – 'he', 'she', 'it', 'his', 'hers', 'they', 'theirs' and so on.

Note the differences:

When I was ten my family moved from Dublin to London.
My father wanted me to be a doctor.

When he was ten his family moved from Dublin to London.
His father wanted him to be a doctor.

Although narratives can be written in either the first or the third person, an autobiography is always written in the first person and a biography is usually written in the third person.
A first person biography may, however, be written when the writer knows the subject personally and is showing how that person has influenced or has affected the writer's own life.

Punctuation pointers

Capital letters

The children will be aware that capital letters are used to begin sentences. Remind them that they are also used for proper nouns:

> Names of people – *Ernest Shackleton*
> Places – *Elephant Island*
> Dates – *January*
> Special names – *The Endurance*

They are also often used for titles and headings, although only the main words begin with a capital letter while conjunctions, prepositions and articles remain lower case. For example:

> *The Early Years*
> *Fourth and Final Expedition*

> The children's version of these notes is on page 25 of the Resource book.

Writing features
Writing chronologically

A biography lends itself to chronological writing and most biographies deal with the subject's life from beginning to end (or to the present day).

It is perfectly acceptable, however, to begin the story at the height of the subject's career or achievement, and detail his life through a series of flashbacks.

The opening

The opening is very important as it sets the tone for the rest of the story. It should be written in a lively way that immediately captures the reader's attention, impresses him and makes him want to read on.

Consider beginning with:

- an exciting event in the subject's life
- telling briefly of his main achievement
- explaining how the subject may have overcome hardship and difficulties to reach his goals
- comments or opinions on his character and/or his achievements (this could include a notable quote)
- an anecdote.

The opening may simply give details of the subject's start in life.

The central section of the biography should be written in chronological order, although some aspects will require more detail than others. This will depend upon the availability of information and how much of interest occurred during a particular period of the subject's life.

Childhood to adulthood

This section should give details of the subject's background, his family and where he spent his early years.

Consider how his developing character traits may have influenced his later career or prepared him for future challenges. Consider also, whether he may have been influenced by others at this time. It may be that ideas for his future were beginning to take shape.

Young adulthood/maturity

In this section the writer deals with major events that take place during the subject's adult life: his career, his discoveries, his adventures and so on. If the subject is well known, the writer will detail the achievements for which he became famous.

Conclusion

The biography may simply end with the death of the subject, but consider:

- summing up the life and work of the subject
- showing how his life affected others
- giving people's comments and opinions of his work.

Each aspect of the subject's life should be carefully linked to show progression.

There are helpful hints for children for writing a biography on page 28 of the Resource book.

Informal Letters

Letter writing has long served as an important means of communication. As long ago as 3500BC, Sumerians sent 'letters' written on cuneiform tablets in clay 'envelopes' and since that time it has become a trusted and effective means of communication in the civilised world. Letter writing really flourished in Europe in the seventeenth century. People needed to exchange information for both official and personal purposes and sending letters became the only reliable means of doing so. The other main source of imparting information, newspapers, was not widely available until the early eighteenth century.

As public postal services were established, so letter writing increased dramatically and was regarded as a rather glamorous pastime.

The following centuries saw the postal service widely used and letters were mailed from region to region and from country to country. It became the most efficient method of dealing with business and of keeping in contact with friends and loved ones.

Today, with the use of advanced communication methods – telephone, fax, email and telephone text messaging – a letter is still the only way for us to express a personal style and to convey our thoughts, ideas, wishes and opinions clearly, concisely and correctly in our own individual way.

Letter writing is a skill that children are likely to need at some point in their lives, whether it be a business letter, a letter of complaint, a letter to a newspaper, a letter of appreciation or simply a way of keeping in touch. But beyond the usefulness of the skill, informal letter writing makes an enjoyable task and gives children experience of writing for different purposes and for different audiences.

Matching writing appropriately to an audience is most important. For example, fashionable jargon and slang may be suitable for letters written to peers but a letter addressed to a grandparent or an older relative would need to be written warmly, but in standard English, and the tone would need to be modified accordingly.

Like diaries, letters are personal and individual and can be very pleasant to write and, of course, especially enjoyable to receive!

Informal letters

Examples of informal letters

Dear Daniel: Letters from Antarctica by Sara Wheeler (Hodder Wayland)
Letters from a Mouse by Herbie Brennan (Walker Books)
Letters to Henrietta by N Marshall (Cambridge University Press)
Simone's Letters by H Pielichaty (Oxford University Press)
Skinny Melon and Me by Jean Ure (Collins)
The Deathwood Letters by Hazel Townson (Red Fox)
The Father Christmas Letters by J R R Tolkein (Harper Collins)

For older readers:

Daddy Long Legs by Jean Webster (Puffin)

The children's illustrated version of the letter is on page 35 of the Resource book.

A letter to Ben

50 Harts Lane
Norford
NF17 4BC[1]

Wednesday 21 November[2]

Dear Ben,[3]

How's things?[4] I can't believe it; I missed your birthday! Did you have a good day and get loadsa cool[5] presents? I hear you went to that new theme park, the one with really scary rides. What was it like? Was it good?[6] You'll have to tell me all about it when we meet up.

Now I'm[7] sending your birthday present – a bit late. It's[7] the latest book by R J Stephen; I know you love his books so I thought it'd[7] be a good choice. If you open the cover, though – guess what! You'll see I got you a signed copy! Aren't I great? I'll tell you how I managed to get it, yeah?[8]

Do you remember me telling you about that writing competition I entered at school last term? You know; the one where we had to write about 'The Most Annoying Member of Your Family', and I wrote about YOU? Well, after the entries were sent off, I totally forgot about it and what with the summer holidays in between, I never gave it another thought.

Until...[9] I was summoned to Mrs Hardcastle's (my headmistress) office. I thought I was in trouble yet again and was standing outside in the corridor, just going over in my mind all the bad things I had done, when she opened the door with a huge smile on her face! To cut a long story short,[10] my piece of writing had been chosen as the regional winner.

I was wowed![11] I mean, can you believe it? I think what really must have done it, was writing about the time when you came to stay. Do you remember?[12] And you decided to take some scissors to my ponytail when I was asleep? Somehow you thought I would look good with a 'David Beckham' cut! Mum didn't think so though, did she? Maybe the judges thought it was amusing![13]

'So what was my prize?' You may ask.[14] A new computer? A stereo sound system? A play station? A stash of cash? No – not quite.[15] But I was invited to a special reception in a posh London hotel to meet the other prize-winners and the judges and to collect my prize – wicked![16]

So last Saturday was the big day. Up early, deciding what to wear – I had to impress! And then off to catch the 8:30 train. Mum came with me – I think she was more excited than I was and she told everyone we met – and I mean everyone, the man at the ticket desk included – that I'd won a major competition and I was off to London to collect my prize![17]

1	Own address in top right hand corner.
2	Date written in full gives good impression.
3	Recipient of letter on next line next to margin.
4	Informal language.
5	Slang.
6	Asking of questions – shows interest in the reader.
7	Use of shortened forms – typical of informal language.
8	Tells the reader what the main body of the letter is about.
9	Use of ellipsis to express anticipation.
10	Cuts out unnecessary detail and moves on to the main point of the letter.
11	use of 'wow' as verb is slang.
12	Draws the reader into the letter by addressing him directly.
13	Use of an anecdote to add interest and humour to the letter.
14	Rhetorical question.
15	Creating interest by hinting that the prize is not too wonderful but is not yet giving details.
16	Slang.
17	Gives insight into Mum's character by telling an anecdote.

When we got to the hotel, it was amazing – all gold and glittery, glass chandeliers and gleaming marble[18]. It reminded me a bit of that ballroom scene in Cinderella.[19] I felt really special – flashbulbs were popping[20] and people were talking to me and asking me questions as if I were really famous. One lady, I can't remember her name, but she introduced herself as one of the judges, asked me if you were still talking to me after what I'd written about you. Ha! Ha! If she knew you and all the horrid stuff you do, she'd wonder why I still speak to you! Which reminds me – did you ever get away with that really cunning trick on your dad? Did he go mad?[21]

Anyway, back to my story. There were the usual speeches about the 'high quality of entries' in this year's competition etc. and then we, the eight regional winners, were called up one by one to collect our prizes… wait for it…. book tokens![22] Great! Just what I wanted![23] Although I think the school was pretty pleased with the £100 I brought back for the library.

I wasn't chosen as national winner – that honour went to some geek[24] who, I think, qualified as the most annoying person himself. He kept going on about his 'new' bike, his 'new' house, his 'new' swimming pool. Yuk! I hope he enjoys his 'new' hand-held computer!

We had some slap-up nosh[25]; every sort of food imaginable and then I spent some time swapping 'annoying' stories with the other winners, although mine were definitely the most impressive!

Anyway, just as we thought the party was over and we were making plans to leave, one of the organisers announced that he had a surprise for us and you'll never guess what… He[26] introduced the author R J Stephen who was going to speak to us. He was really interesting; he told us a bit about how he started writing, and about his latest book and then he talked about the film they've made from his book, 'Whatever Happened to Wizards?' Now that's a film we gotta see![27]

After his talk he signed copies of his book for us. He was so cool! He said he'd read my competition entry – loved my description and he asked if he could include my character i.e. you, in his next book![29] So, cousin dear, you may become famous yet!

I thought it only right that you should have the signed copy since, without you, I'd never have won the prize![30] So enjoy it. And write back soon and tell me what you think of it.

Keep out of trouble.[31]

Love

Jessica

18 Use of alliteration to aid description.

19 Short description but sums up Jessica's impressions of the hotel.

20 Use of the active makes writing more interesting, rather than the passive 'My photo was taken'.

21 Brings the focus back to the recipient of the letter by asking another question; this time probably requesting a reply.

22 Use of ellipses.

23 Sarcasm.

24 Slang.

25 Slang.

26 Ellipsis.

27 Brings the reader in again. Also emphasis of 'that's'.

29 An added and unexpected twist.

30 Brings the letter full circle – back to the purpose of writing.

31 Casual and light-hearted signing off.

Understanding the grammar and punctuation

Understanding the grammar and punctuation enables children to control the language they use and therefore to write more effectively.

Grammar pointers

Help the children to be more aware of the following when writing their letters.

Slang

Slang is informal language and is mainly used in conversation. It is considered to be outside standard English and is therefore less suitable for written work, except in dialogue and letters to close friends. Slang is an important part of language and almost everyone uses it daily. It helps to keep the language lively by introducing new words and giving old words an injection of new meaning and it can add humour and variety to language. However, slang can easily and quickly become out of date and overuse of a slang term will make it sound stale. Some words that were once considered slang are now part of standard English, such as bus, mob and blizzard.

Discuss the following.

Did you have a good day and get loadsa cool presents?

That honour went to some geek.

In the first example, the word 'loadsa' is slang for 'loads of'.

In the second example, the word 'geek' is a slang term meaning 'an intelligent but socially inept person'.

In using these terms, the writer can relate easily and quickly to a reader who is of a similar age and from a similar background. Slang usage, however, can change from area to area and even from school to school.

It is important to note that much of today's slang will have little meaning to an older generation.

Punctuation pointers

Using apostrophes

There are two ways to use the apostrophe:
* to indicate omission
* to indicate possession

Omission

Remind the children that apostrophes are used to show that a letter or letters have been missed out when writing shortened forms. For example:

I will becomes *I'll* and *do not* becomes *don't.*

Often children believe that an apostrophe goes where the two words join instead of where the letters are missing. For example:

does'nt – this is WRONG

doesn't – this is RIGHT

But if they can remember why an apostrophe is used they should remember where it goes.

Possession

Apostrophes are used to show that something belongs to someone or something. For example:

Jessica's prize – the prize belonging to Jessica

Remind the children of the rules:

* When something belongs to a single person or thing, add an apostrophe and 's'.

  the boy's computer

* If the word already ends in 's', then you can either just add an apostrophe after the 's' or add an apostrophe and an 's'. Both are right.

  James' presents
  James's presents

* When something belongs to more than one person or thing, add an apostrophe after the 's'.

  the prize-winners' book tokens

* If the plural form of the word does not end in 's' add an apostrophe and 's'.

  the children's stories

* Belonging to 'it' does not follow the same rule.

  its – belonging to it
  it's – it is

> The children's version of these notes is on page 38 of the Resource book.

Writing features
Layout, structure and audience

Private letters, like diaries, are personal documents not intended for publication, but observation of some of the conventions of informal writing makes for more interesting and lively letter writing.

Layout

Make sure the children are familiar with the layout of an informal letter:
- Own address at the top right-hand corner with the date underneath. Remind them that unlike formal letters, there is no need to include the recipient's address.
- Dear … on the next line and against the left-hand margin and then the body of the letter beneath this.
- Informal ending , for example 'Love from' for family or close friends and 'Best wishes' for other people. Only the first name is needed for signature since the reader will obviously know the writer well.
- Paragraphs to be used to introduce new elements but ideas should be linked by the use of discourse markers, for example 'That's not all…', 'On the other hand..' or 'However…'

Stress the importance of clear, neat handwriting so that the letter is legible and attractive to the reader.

Structure

Explain to the children that the most successful letters are planned in logical order. It is very easy to lose control of the writing by including unrelated and haphazard thoughts and ideas. Writing clearly and in detail about two or three ideas or incidents is much more effective and will keep the reader interested.

Jokes or humorous comments can add liveliness to writing but they should be appropriate to the subject and should not cause offence. Anecdotal tales will make a worthwhile addition. For example in Jessica's letter she tells the story of Ben cutting her hair whilst she was asleep.

Many informal letters contain mundane, everyday matters, such as what was on television, what was for dinner and Grandad coming to tea, so any element of surprise or excitement will add interest and supplement the content.

Writing for an audience

As with all writing, it is important to match it appropriately to the audience. Explain to the children that they need to target their audience and tailor their writing accordingly by:
- the type of language they use
- the tone of the letter
- the subject matter.

It is acceptable to use fashionable jargon or slang when writing to peers, but when addressing an older relative or friend it is wiser to use standard English. For example, in the model, Jessica uses the words 'loadsa' and 'geek' – terms which may be unfamiliar to an older generation. The tone of her letter may also seem a little disrespectful to adults.

The subject content should aim to interest the reader and may need to be modified according to the age and/or relationship of the reader.

There are helpful hints for children for writing an informal letter on page 41 of the Resource book.

Formal letters

In today's world of advanced communications – telephone, fax, email and telephone messaging, many consider letter writing a dying art. However, the ability to write a letter that is carefully constructed and well presented will prove to be a worthwhile lifetime skill for any child.

Letters fall into two main categories – informal and formal. Unit 3 gives ideas on writing informal letters with the emphasis on an accepted layout and the need for clarity of purpose and organisation.

In this unit the children will be introduced to the skills of writing for official purposes. There are a number of letter types. For example:

- To inform – for example, to give information about products, services, prices and availability.
- To protest – for example, about the treatment of animals or the closure of amenities.
- To complain – for example, about faulty goods or poor service.
- To persuade – for example, the local council to provide better services or people to donate money to a charity.
- To give an opinion – for example, views on a television programme or a newspaper article.

The aim is to extend and enhance children's existing writing knowledge by studying and preparing formats for formal letters, specifically for the purposes of complaining, informing and persuading.

They will learn the correct presentation and the use of appropriate styles and tones of correspondence according to the purpose of their letters. They will also investigate formal language and build upon their own vocabulary to compose letters that are precise, efficient and businesslike.

Formal letters

Examples of formal letters

School to parents informing them of school events.

Medical/dental practices giving details of appointments.

Banks, building societies and so on, giving information about their services and persuading the reader to invest.

Charities and fund-raising committees requesting donations.

Local councils and governments canvassing votes or giving information about a wide range of local issues.

Shops, stores, garages and so on, persuading the reader to buy their goods.

Also – letters to newspapers and magazines expressing opinions on current issues.

The children may be able to add to this list.

The children's versions of the following formal letters are on pages 48–50 of the Resource book.

A letter to complain

Wensum Cottage
Bridge Road
Whitton
Herts
SR7 3PM[1]

24th December 2001[2]

The Manager
Star Cinema
Broad Street
Newtown
Herts
NT3 5GB[3]

Dear Sir or Madam[4]

I am writing to express my dissatisfaction with the service offered by your staff on my recent visit to your cinema.[5]

On Sunday 23rd December, I took my grandchildren to see the latest 'Harry Potter' film. Unfortunately, we were unable to fully enjoy the showing as we were evacuated from the cinema approximately twenty minutes before the end, apparently because of a technical problem.[6]

Whilst I am aware that the circumstances, which resulted in the evacuation, were beyond your control, I am disappointed with the way your staff handled the matter.[7]

When the alarm sounded, a recorded message advised us to leave the building by the nearest available exit. There was little sense of urgency from members of your staff and the arrangements for emergency evacuation seemed woefully inadequate.[8] We were left, standing outside in the cold night air[9], for at least forty minutes and without any explanation.

Eventually,[10] we learned by word of mouth that the sprinkler system had been tampered with, and that the fire service and technicians were working in the building. At no time were we officially informed[11] of the situation or told whether it would be possible to resume the showing of the film. Any attempts to request information were met by unhelpful comments from your staff.

After a further[10] twenty minutes of waiting, and with no clear explanation or apology for the inconvenience, we decided to leave.

As you can imagine, my grandchildren were not only bored and cold, but also extremely disappointed to have missed the end of a long awaited film.[12]

I would appreciate, therefore, a full refund for the cost of the tickets. I would also suggest that you review your health and safety procedures and in future train your staff to adopt a more courteous and reassuring manner with your customers.[13]

I trust that this matter will receive your prompt attention.[14]

Yours faithfully[15]

J. Finch

Mrs. J. Finch[16]

1. The writer's address in top right-hand corner. There is no need to use commas or full stops in the address.

2. Date written under writer's address.

3. Address of recipient of letter on next line next to left margin.

4. The writer does not know the name or sex of the manager and so uses the titles 'Sir or Madam'.

5. Opening sentence clearly states purpose of letter using formal term '...express my dissatisfaction' rather than 'I'm not happy with'.

6. Example of complex sentence. (Much of the letter is written in complex sentences.) Note the use of commas to help the reader make sense of a complex sentence.

7. Complex sentence using formal language. 'Whilst I am aware that the circumstances ... beyond your control' meaning, 'I know you couldn't do anything about it'. Note the use of commas to enclose the relative subordinate clause – 'which resulted in the evacuation'. In formal letters the full form of words, rather than shortened forms, are used. So 'I am', not 'I'm'.

8. Formal language meaning 'pretty hopeless'.

9. Subordinate clause beginning with a verb.

10. Words and phrases such as 'eventually' and 'after a further ...' link paragraphs. A comma is used after many connecting adverbs.

11. Another example of formal language – 'nobody told us'.

12. This paragraph sums up the message. The writer adopts a reasonable tone rather than being aggressive.

13. Explains, in a polite but firm manner, what action the writer would like to be taken to rectify the situation.

14. Finishes with a simple sentence formally asking the manager to deal with the complaint quickly.

15. The writer does not know the name of the recipient so she signs off with 'Yours faithfully'.

16. The writer's name is written legibly beneath the signature.

A letter to inform

Wonderbike Ltd
22 The Place
Bedminster
Hants
BD7 6GS[1]

16th July 2001[2]

Miss G Fairhurst
10 New Road
Rockington
Hants
RG4 3SP[3]

Dear Miss Fairhurst

It is a great pleasure to inform you that you have won first prize in the 'Name the Bicycle' competition[4] with your entry 'The Mighty Merlin'. This entitles you[5] to the prize of a bicycle of your choice from our new range of exclusive cycles.

We would like to invite you to a presentation evening at 6.30 pm on Friday 3rd August at our showroom at the above address.[6] We expect the press to be in attendance and that your photograph will appear in the local newspaper. The evening will be informal and we hope you will[7] be able to bring a guest with you.

The standard of entries was very high and the judges were impressed, not only with the suitability of the name, but also with your slogan, 'The Mighty Merlin is a Magical Machine'[8].

I would like to congratulate you on your success and I look forward to seeing you on 2nd August.[9]

Yours sincerely[10]

J Jones

J. Jones (Manager)[11]

---

1   The writer's address in top right-hand corner.

2   Date written under writer's address.

3   Address of recipient of letter on next line next to left margin.

4   Opening sentence clearly states purpose of letter.

5   Formal language meaning 'you can have'.

6   Second paragraph gives details of claiming the prize.

7   In formal letters the full forms of words rather than shortened forms are used.

8   Complex sentence. Note use of commas to aid the sense of the sentence.

9   The final paragraph sums up the message of the letter.

10 The writer knows the name of the recipient so he signs off with 'Yours sincerely'.

11 The writer's name and status are written clearly under the signature.

A letter to persuade

9 Bloomfield Road
Camford
W. Yorks
CM14 3BY[1]

17 January 2002[2]

Mr. V. Bidewell
St John's School
Park Drive
Camford
W. Yorks
CM9 6CZ[3]

Dear Mr Bidewell[4]

I am writing on behalf of class 6F to ask you whether you would consider allowing us to have a Charities Week towards the end of this academic year.[5]

I am aware that the school does raise money for charity throughout the year, but we feel that if we concentrated our efforts into one week, the benefits to both the pupils and the charities would be considerable.[6]

Our aim would be to have various fund-raising activities throughout the week, culminating in a Charity Fayre on the Friday afternoon. This would mean that everybody would be entirely focused on charity work during that particular week rather than making sporadic fund-raising efforts at different times during the year. We feel sure that this would result in a vast increase in the money raised.

I can assure you that children really do care about people less fortunate than ourselves and we are very keen to raise the largest amount of money we can[7]. This year we would like to support the charities Save the Children and Help the Aged.

We have a number of proposals for the venture[8], including a 'Line of Pennies', a 'Non-uniform Day' and a 'Teddy Bears' Picnic'. Year 6 pupils would have the responsibility for the organisation of the project and we anticipate needing only the minimum of adult help and supervision.

The majority of events will take place during lunch breaks so that they do not encroach on lesson time[9]. The exception to this will be the Friday afternoon Fayre. We envisage that this will be organised solely by the pupils themselves[9] and groups of children from different classes will supervise games such as 'Guess How Many Sweets are in the Jar' or 'Find the Treasure'. We hope that the whole school will be able to visit the Fayre during the afternoon and spend their money.

We are sure that the benefits arising from such a venture will compensate for any lost curriculum time.[10]

We hope, therefore, that you will be able to support our ideas and that you will give us positive feedback[11] in the near future.

Yours sincerely[12]

Jasmine Patel

Jasmine Patel[13]

---

1 Own address in top right-hand corner.

2 Date written in full gives good impression.

3 Address of recipient of letter on next line next to left margin.

4 The recipient is addressed by name.

5 Opening paragraph clearly states the reason for writing. The request is very polite –'whether you would consider' rather than 'if we can'.

6 In the second paragraph the writer states valid reasons for her request, which may persuade the reader to her point of view. In the next paragraph she reinforces her view.

7 The writer adopts a persuasive tone by expressing a sympathetic and sincere approach to the cause.

8 Formal, businesslike vocabulary is used for clarity and to give the correct impression to the reader.

9 Both of these statements are designed to persuade the head teacher to agree to the venture.

10 This paragraph sums up the message of the letter and includes a final attempt at persuasion.

11 In the closing paragraph the writer formally asks the head teacher to agree to the request.

12 The recipient's name is known so the term 'Yours sincerely' is used.

13 The writer's name is written legibly beneath her signature.

Understanding the grammar and punctuation

Understanding the grammar and punctuation enables children to control the language they use and therefore to write more effectively.

Grammar pointers

Help the children be aware of the following when writing their letters.

Formal language

Formal language is used for writing official or business letters. It is impersonal in tone so that the reader feels distanced from the writer. The vocabulary is precise and correct. Set phrases are often used. For example:

I am writing to express my dissatisfaction with …

I trust that this matter will receive your prompt attention.

Slang is never used in formal letter writing.

Sentences

A **simple** sentence is composed of one main clause with a single verb.

You are invited to a presentation evening.

A **compound** sentence has two or more clauses joined by a conjunction.

I would like to congratulate you on your success and *I look forward to seeing you on 3rd August.*

A **complex** sentence contains a main clause and one or more subordinate clauses. The subordinate clause provides more information about the main clause.

Unfortunately, we were unable to fully enjoy the showing as we were evacuated from the cinema approximately twenty minutes before the end.

A subordinate clause often starts with a subordinate conjunction – 'as', 'although' or 'while'. The subordinate clause may also begin with a verb.

*Our aim would be to have various fund-raising activities throughout the week, **culminating** in a Charity Fayre on the Friday afternoon.*

When a sentence is made up of two clauses, the clause that comes first is emphasised.

Punctuation pointers

Using commas

Commas are used to make it easier for the reader to follow the sense of a sentence. They are used for the following:

- Before closing speech marks.

  "Thank you for my prize," said Georgina.

- Items in a list are separated by a comma. The last two items are usually separated by 'and'.

  We propose a Non-uniform Day, a Line of Pennies, a Raffle and a Teddy Bears' Picnic.

- To mark off words such as 'please', 'thank you', 'well', 'yes' and 'no' and after conjunctions such as 'however' and 'nevertheless'.

  "Yes, I hope to be able to come to the presentation. However, I will be coming alone."

- A comma is used to separate the name of someone who is being addressed.

  "Miss Fairhurst, congratulations on your success."

- A comma is also used to separate clauses and phrases that are parenthetical or naturally cut off from the sentence.

  Georgina Fairhurst, who was eleven, won first prize.

  In such a sentence the clause within the commas may be removed without altering its meaning.

- A comma is also used to separate clauses and phrases which occur in complex sentences.

  I am aware that the school does raise money for charity throughout the year, but we feel that if we concentrated our efforts into one week, the benefits to both the pupils and the charities would be considerable.

- If the subordinate clause precedes the main clause, it is often followed by a comma.

  Although she won first prize, Georgina was not happy with her slogan.

- Commas may be used to simply indicate pauses in complicated sentences.

  The rule is: Use a comma to indicate a pause where it helps the sense; don't use one where it does not.

> The children's version of these notes is on page 51 of the Resource book.

Writing features
Format, style and tone

Letters written formally are addressed to someone for a specific purpose, such as:

- to inform or ask for information
- to order something
- to criticise or complain about something
- to express dissatisfaction
- to express an opinion
- to congratulate
- to persuade someone to your point of view

The following need to be observed.

Format

Explain to the children that they should use the following format when they want to write to someone on a professional basis or when they want to maintain a formal relationship with the addressee. For instance, it would be highly unlikely they would write a letter to their head teacher in an informal way. The choice of a formal letter would reflect the relationship between the head teacher and themselves; she or he occupies a position of authority and so they would wish to show the necessary respect.

Make sure the children are familiar with the layout of a formal letter:

- Own address in top right-hand corner with date beneath.
- Address of recipient on left-hand side of next line.
- Dear (Sir, Madam or their name if known).
- Paragraphs to state the reason for writing, the details of the letter and the action you want to be taken.
- Formal ending ('Yours faithfully' if the recipient's name is unknown, otherwise 'Yours sincerely').

Style

The style of formal correspondence needs to be clear and crisp. The writer should deliver the message as accurately and completely as possible. She or he should state what he or she wants, keep to the point and include all the important facts.

Encourage the children to use linking phrases and discourse markers, for example 'what is more', 'in addition' and 'without question' to support and

emphasise their viewpoint, and to finish their letters with suitable endings, such as 'I shall look forward to receiving...' or 'I am sure you will wish to consider the matter further...'

Tone

Explain to the children that the tone of a letter reflects the writer's attitude towards the subject matter. It is important to write in the appropriate tone so that the right impression is given to the reader. They should aim to be polite but firm and reasonable in any requests.

In official letters the writer needs to use formal language, in the sense that it needs to be precise, accurate, clear and concise. For example:

informed of the situation

told what was going on

attempt to request information

try to find out what is going on

we hope you will give us positive feedback

we hope you will say "Yes"

seemed woefully inadequate

wasn't good enough

There are helpful hints for children for writing a formal letter on page 54 of the Resource book.

Instructions

Instructions tell people how to perform a procedure or a particular task.

We can expect to respond to written or verbal instructions on numerous occasions in our daily lives. Whether we are following a recipe for a new dish, following directions to get to a place or simply acquiring information for our work or leisure, our success depends upon how well the instructions are given.

There are many times, too, we need to give instructions to others and it can be vital that we communicate our knowledge effectively.

Children are familiar with following oral and written instructions, but they may be less experienced in giving instructions. It is important that they develop not only their verbal skills, but also their written communication skills.

By learning to write in a structured and logical manner, by using a step-by-step procedure and by learning the correct use of grammar, they will be able to write instructions that are clear, concise and useful.

The successful instruction writer needs:

- to define his audience and the purpose of his instructions;
- to be aware of how much the reader will already know about the situation and the process before he begins so that he can target his instructions according to his audience;
- to have a thorough understanding of the procedure, to be able to visualise it in detail, and to try to capture that awareness on paper;
- to put himself in the place of the person who is trying to use the instructions;
- to check that his instructions follow a logical sequence and are unambiguous;
- to keep terminology to the minimum and fully explain unfamiliar terms;
- to use diagrams and illustrations when explaining how to make or assemble items, and these need to be straightforward, clearly labelled and easy to refer to.

Instructions

Examples of instructions

Examples of instructions may be found in a variety of sources familiar to the children. These include:

- recipes;
- directions to places;
- instructions for assembling toys or gadgets;
- care instructions;
- instructions for practical uses for household items;
- instructions for making or constructing objects in design technology;
- instructions for using communication technology – TV, VCR and DVD players, mobile phones, computers and so on;
- rules for games.

The children's illustrated version of the instructional leaflet is on page 62 of the Resource book.

Instructions

Caring for your new puppy[1]

Getting a new puppy is incredibly exciting but it is also a huge commitment. Your puppy will rely on you[2] to provide all its basic needs and it is your responsibility to bring up a healthy and well-trained dog. By careful preparation you can help your puppy settle quickly into its new home.[3]

Equipment[4]

Here is some of the basic equipment you will need to keep your puppy happy and fulfil his needs in the first few weeks of his life with you.

- Bed and bedding
- Food and water bowls
- Food
- Run or playpen
- Toys
- Collar, lead or harness and identity tag
- Brush and comb

Bed and bedding[5]

Provide your puppy with its own special sleeping area. Choose a plastic or soft bed, a wicker basket or even a cardboard box. Bedding can be anything soft and warm – blankets, old towels, woollen sweaters or a specially bought polyester rug. Put his bed in a secluded, draught free place near to a source of heat for winter warmth.

Collar, lead and identity tag[6]

Get your puppy accustomed to wearing a collar and introduce him to a lead. Bear in mind these safety tips about collars.
- Don't expect your puppy to wear anything too heavy, as it will damage his neck.[7]
- Don't fasten it too tightly – you should be able to comfortably slide two fingers between your puppy's neck and collar.
- Don't leave anything sticking out which may catch the collar; it could hang your puppy.

Instead of a lead, a harness could be worn – this will stop your dog pulling with his neck when out walking.

Make sure your puppy wears an identification tag at all times. You may also consider having an identity microchip implanted.

---

1 The title is big and bold making the purpose of the instructions clear.

2 The audience is addressed directly.

3 Introductory paragraph reiterates the purpose of the instructions.

4 The information regarding equipment required is set out in a box for easy access.

5 Layout of these instructions is a series of subheadings followed by short paragraphs of information.

6 There is no logical order to the information so the subheadings are set out alphabetically.

7 Bullet points within the paragraph are used for emphasis.

Food and water

<u>You will need</u>[8] separate dishes for food and water. Fresh water must be available to your puppy at all times.

Find out what food your puppy has been eating and continue with this diet until he has settled into your home. <u>Introduce any new foods gradually.</u>[9]

<u>Puppies are usually fed</u>[10] three times a day until they are six months old, then two feeds a day until they are nine months. Always give food in the dog's own bowl and never offer titbits when you are eating, as this will encourage begging.

Grooming

<u>Your puppy will need his own brush and comb and if he has long hair, a special pair of trimming scissors. Brush your dog every day to remove dust and dead hair, and bath your dog whenever he is particularly dirty or smelly. Most dogs need bathing just twice a year. Overbathing can dry out your dog's coat and strip away the natural waterproofing. Always use a special dog shampoo and avoid the puppy's eyes, ears and mouth.</u>[11]

House-training

<u>Begin house-training</u>[12] your puppy as soon as you bring him home for the first time. <u>Introduce him</u>[12] to the place in the garden that will be his toilet area. A verbal command, such as 'Toilet', should be used as soon as possible. If said often enough, the puppy will connect the word with the action.

<u>Establish a set routine</u>[12]. <u>Feed him</u>[12] at the same time each day and take him to the toilet area afterwards. <u>Give him</u>[12] the opportunity of using the toilet every two hours. <u>Praise him</u>[12] lavishly when he performs!

House-training won't take place overnight and a few accidents around the house are to be expected. House-training takes time, patience and understanding.

Obedience

Start training your puppy at 8 – 12 weeks. It usually takes about three months to train a puppy. Train only for a few minutes at a time, twice daily when your puppy is alert.

Train your puppy to come, sit, lie down and stay down. These obedience skills are important for both the puppy's safety and socialising. Always accompany a verbal command with a hand signal and never shout or use physical punishment. Even a young puppy will be sensitive to your manner and tone of voice and will understand when you are genuinely pleased with his behaviour. Offer lots of praise when your puppy obeys your command.

Run or playpen

Use a playpen, cage or run when it is inconvenient to have your puppy under your feet. It can keep your puppy safe and teach him to play on his own.

8 The future tense is used quite commonly when writing instructions.

9 Use of simple sentences makes important points clearly understood and leaves no room for ambiguity.

10 Most instructions are written in the present tense.

11 Linking sentences in a paragraph gives the opportunity to link ideas effectively.

12 Use of the imperative form of the verb makes it clear what the reader should do. The imperative often comes at the beginning of the sentence.

Toys

All puppies need toys to help stimulate their minds and bodies. If provided with proper toys, a teething puppy will chew on these rather than the furniture, wallpaper or socks! Make sure the toys you choose are non-toxic, have no detachable small parts and cannot be swallowed.

Place a soft toy with the puppy at night for extra comfort.[13]

Walking

Ensure that walking with your dog is a pleasure by teaching him from an early age to walk to heel.

Make sure that when you walk your puppy in public, he is under control and on a lead or harness. Don't avoid other dogs. Once he has been vaccinated, your puppy needs to develop his social skills.

Your puppy should be happy with two good walks every day especially if time is made for some off lead exercise.

****

If you follow these guidelines, you will have a healthy, happy and well-trained dog that will make an ideal companion and give you many years of pleasure.[14]

13 The language is suitable for the target audience – in this instance, for both children and adults.

14 The concluding paragraph rounds off the instructions and reinforces their purpose.

Understanding the grammar and punctuation

Understanding the grammar and punctuation enables children to control the language they use and therefore to write effectively.

Grammar pointers

Verbs

Remind the children that a verb is usually essential to the structure of a sentence. It is most concerned with the action and is often known as the 'doing' word.

A sentence may only have a main verb like 'is' or 'was' or 'go'. Or it may consist of a main verb and an auxiliary verb like 'has been', 'shall go' or 'will be'.

> When your puppy _obeys_ your command ... (main verb)

> Your puppy _will rely_ on you ... (auxiliary + main verb)

Tenses

The tense of a verb tells you when the action is taking place. There are three main tenses. What is happening now is in the present tense; what has happened is in the past tense; what is still to happen is in the future tense.

Auxiliary verbs are used to form different tenses. The most common are the verb 'to be':

> When your puppy _is_ teething, it will chew everything! (present)

> Find out what sort of bed your puppy _was_ sleeping in. (past)

> Your puppy _will_ need feeding three times a day. (future)

and the verb 'to have':

> When your puppy _has_ eaten, give him the opportunity of using the toilet. (past)

The imperative

The word derives from the Latin 'imperare' which means 'to order'. When we use verbs as commands, they are said to be in the imperative. For example:

> _Establish_ a set routine.
> _Feed_ him three times a day.
> _Praise_ him when he performs.

The imperative form needs no subject or pronoun in front of it. It implies that you need to do something but the 'you' is left out. It is used to:
- ask or tell someone to do something;
- give advice or a warning;
- give instructions on how to do something.

Punctuation pointers

Layout punctuation

Sometimes punctuation is an important part of the layout. If a number of facts or statements are emphasised by separating them into a list, the punctuation is often as follows:

- the items in the list will start with a lower case letter;
- the end of each item will have a semicolon;
- the last item will have a full stop.

The reason for this is that a colon, not a full stop, follows the word 'follows'. Therefore the three separate items are not discrete sentences, but phrases within a sentence, which is finished at the end of the last item. This applies if the list is indicated by bullet points as above, by letters or by numerals.

The children's version of these notes is on page 66 of the Resource book.

Writing features
Organisation methods

Explain to the children that they will need to identify their audience and the purpose of their instructions. They will also need to plan their instructions so that they are written in a clear and logical order.

Ideas should be organised within a general structure and points arranged in sections. These could be:

- chronological order – beginning with the step people need to follow first and then proceeding sequentially until the final instruction;
- order of importance – beginning with the most important point and moving on to subsequent instructions;
- alphabetical order – listing points alphabetically when there is no other specific order to the instructions.

The children will need to decide which layout device to use. This will vary according to the audience and the nature of the instructions. The instructions could be set out as:

- a numbered list of points;
- subheadings with bullet points;
- subheadings with paragraphs;
- continuous writing.

Numbered points and bullets

It is easier to follow instructions when they are laid out clearly in points. This method is especially useful when writing instructions for 'How to make a ...' or 'Assembling a ...' The step-by-step organisation leaves little room for confusion.

Subheadings with paragraphs

Using subheadings followed by short paragraphs gives the opportunity to write more detailed instructions. In the model, the instructions for 'Caring for your new puppy' provide more information for the reader than simply a list of points. The use of headed paragraphs makes the information more readily accessible.

Continuous writing

When giving instructions in the form of a continuous piece of writing, it is important to write very clearly and succinctly in order to avoid confusion. This method is suitable when writing instructions to explain a situation or event, for example a guide to holidaying abroad or the format for a meeting or school trip.

It is vital to use discourse markers, such as 'Then...', 'Next...', 'Following this...', 'It is essential that...', 'After you have...', 'Above all...' and 'The next stage...'

It may be appropriate to begin with an introduction to the subject indicating what areas will be covered. For example, in 'Caring for your new puppy' the opening paragraph explains that by following the instructions you will 'help your puppy settle quickly into its new home'.

Similarly, a conclusion will round off your writing. For example, 'If you follow these guidelines, you will have a healthy, happy and well-trained 'dog that will make an ideal companion and give you many years of pleasure.'

The children may also wish to draw up a dos and don'ts box at the end to summarise the main points.

There are helpful hints for children for writing instructions on page 69 of the Resource book.

Leaflets and advertisements

Persuasive leaflets and advertisements encourage people to buy products or services, donate money, attend events or support causes. Although the aims of the leaflet or product may differ, many persuasive leaflets or advertisements use similar features.

Headlines or captions

The headline is read by more people than the copy. It is therefore a miniature advertisement to summarise the message for those who read no further. Effective headlines:

- are eye-catching and dominate the page;
- are bold and clearly written so they are quick and easy to read;
- promise some benefit;
- use powerful language.

Copy

This is usually in smaller print and is set out in columns or chunks. It may be quite lengthy but it is important to include all the information about the product or cause. Paragraphs are kept short and the language is simple.

Text boxes

Facts, opinions or statistics may be placed in boxes to stand out from the rest of the text. There are usually only one or two of these boxes per page and they are used for maximum visual impact.

Illustrations

These may be photographs, drawings or cartoons and are very important in catching the reader's attention and inducing him/her to spend more time reading the entire advertisement. Often, stereotypes are used because they are easily recognisable to the reader.

Emotive language

Advertisers will use 'loaded' or 'emotive' language to appeal to the reader's senses and may even use emotive pictures and vocabulary to make the reader feel sad or guilty in the hope they will donate money.

A successful piece of persuasive writing needs to have a clear sense of purpose; needs to target a specific audience and should be direct and focused.

Advertisements

Examples of advertisements

Advertising is all around us. Look for advertisements:

- in magazines and newspapers;
- on hoardings;
- on product packaging;
- on TV, radio and the Internet;
- on public transport;
- in shops.

The children's illustrated versions of the leaflet and advertisements are on pages 76–79 of the Resource book.

A leaflet

CHOOSE THE CHARNWELL CHALLENGE[1]

At Charnwell Activity Centre <u>your pupils</u>[2] will benefit from the <u>best possible learning environment</u>.[3] They will be fully challenged; they will acquire new skills and above all they will have fun!

WHY CHARNWELL?[4]

Good for the children[5]

The <u>challenge</u>[6] of spending a few fun-filled days away from home and family increases the children's self-sufficiency and builds confidence. For many, it will be their first taste of freedom and responsibility. <u>Your pupils will learn to live and work together, trust and rely on each other and share in the sense of achievement that success creates.</u>[7]

Our promise:

- self-confidence
- independence
- initiative
- achievement

Good for the teacher

Organising a trip to Charnwell couldn't be easier. Our friendly staff are here to help you from the moment you pick up the phone until the moment your visit ends.

***

<u>Our programme of events is designed to support your teaching in the classroom.</u>[8]

***

Many teachers find that the benefits of a visit to Charnwell are enormous. It gives them an opportunity to view their pupils in a different light and to discover their strengths and their qualities.

Our staff

Our instructors are young, enthusiastic and extensively trained in the techniques of active learning. They are trained to take responsibility for the wellbeing of each and every child.

With our high staff–pupil ratio we are able to offer a warm and supportive environment all the time.

---

1   The title is emboldened. Alliteration is used to make the title more memorable. Double meaning on the word 'challenge' – we challenge you to come to Charnwell and the children will be challenged. The theme 'challenge' is used throughout the leaflet.

2   The opening paragraph sets out the purpose and the audience – in this case, teachers.

3   Opinion disguised as fact.

4   Rhetorical question leads the reader into the main message.

5   Subheadings guide the reader through the information.

6   Emotive word 'challenge'. The word is repeated several times in the leaflet – for emphasis.

7   The leaflet begins in quite a formal tone to make the message appear authoritative.

8   Information is given in chunks to make it easily accessible. There are short paragraphs and simple sentences.

Our campus

Our centre is situated in a lovely tranquil woodland setting on the banks of the River Warne and very close to the seashore. The site abounds with wildlife to discover and nearby are rocky cliffs and long sandy beaches to explore.[9]

The children stay in comfortable warm[10] log cabins that accommodate four to six children. All have en-suite facilities, and snug duvets[10] and clean linen are supplied.

The central dining room provides three hearty meals each day with plenty of choice.[11] There are also opportunities for drinks throughout the day.

12

Safety

Safety at Charnwell is paramount. We[13] have a superb reputation for quality and safety. All possible precautions are taken with nothing left to chance. Qualified nursing staff are on site at all times and all our[13] instructors are trained in first aid. Our[13] site is secure[14] and staff are on duty 24 hours a day.

ADVENTURE CHALLENGE[15]

We have extremely spacious grounds and can accommodate a vast number of outdoor activities. We also have a purpose-built sports centre for all indoor activities and for use in cold or wet weather.

All our activities are designed to challenge the children in a personal way and are very varied. Here is a selection of what we offer:

Water sports

We make full use of our unique[16] position and canoeing and kayaking take place on the river or at the coast. We have our own exceptional[16] swimming pool and here the youngsters learn the art of capsizing before taking to the waters. Other activities include dragon boat racing, rafting and swimming.

Climbing and abseiling

Climbing is a real challenge requiring strength, coordination and nerve. The sense of achievement when children reach the summit of a climbing wall is difficult to beat.

Abseiling down a tower for the first time is probably one of the most memorable experiences of the visit and is the most popular activity.[17]

---

9   Images created give an almost fairytale quality to the description – used for persuasive effect.

10 Emotive vocabulary evokes feelings of security and warmth.

11 Tone becomes less formal.

12 Picture for visual impact – helps to get message across.

13 Pronouns 'we' and 'our' are used as a persuasive device to indicate togetherness.

14 Use of the present tense throughout.

15 Use of the word 'challenge' again – coupled with 'adventure' to give appealing image.

16 Use of powerful adjectives to make the product appear perfect.

17 Opinion or fact?

Initiative exercises

These are designed to promote life skills, raise self-esteem and build self-confidence.[18] *Initiative exercises such as orienteering, raft building and low ropes all help to forge team spirit and develop leadership skills.*

Challenge yourself[19]

- kayaking
- abseiling
- climbing
- mountain biking
- dragon boat racing
- quad biking

Motor sports

We have purpose-built dirt tracks where the children can safely[20] *try their hands at quad bike racing and driving go-karts and buggies. Here the children can experience the thrill of being in control of their own motor vehicle while under strict supervision.*

All our activities will be designed in consultation with school staff and may include:

aeroball   archery   caving   fencing   night hikes

SO WHY CHARNWELL?[21]

Don't rely on us to answer the question.[22] Here's what fellow teachers have to say:[23]

'The children had a marvellous[24] *time. They loved the food, the activities – everything!'*

'A brilliant[24] *trip! Thanks to all the staff!'*

'Excellent[24] *experience for the kids – great diversity of activities.'*

If you would like to take up the Charnwell challenge[25]**, contact us at:**
Charnwell Activity Centre
Charnwell House
Warne Road
Charnwell
Tel: 013529 749003
email: enquiries@charnwell.co.uk
Website: www.charnwell.co.uk[26]

---

18 A return to more formal language - used to emphasise serious qualities of the product.

19 Text box highlights more adventurous activities. The word 'challenge' is used again. Bullet points make it easier to read.

20 The word 'safely' is used to appeal to teachers – shows a sense of responsibility.

21 Rhetorical question echoes the original question and is used to sum up the message.

22 Addresses the reader directly using the imperative form of the verb.

23 Uses others' opinions to influence the reader.

24 Powerful adjectives used. Exclamation marks used for emphasis.

25 Persuasive device – invitation to the reader. Could be used as a slogan.

26 Contact address. It is important to include all information.

ADIKE

THE LEGEND[3]
Introduces the latest!

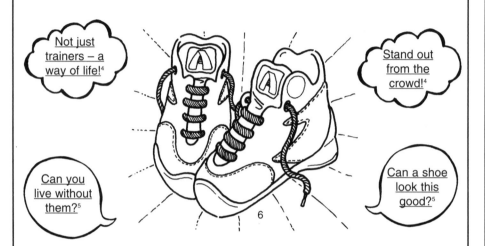

Not just trainers – a way of life![4]

Stand out from the crowd![4]

Can you live without them?[5]

Can a shoe look this good?[5]

6

THE
ULTIMATE![7]

Stay on track[8] with ADIKE!!!

ADIKE – Moving to a different beat!!

THEY'RE STYLISH
THEY'RE SMOOTH
THEY'RE STRONG
THEY'RE SENSATIONAL[9]
THEY'RE SO WORTH IT![10]

13

NEW![11]
IN SPORTS SHOPS
NOW

WIN![12]
TWO WORLD CUP
TICKETS FOR NEW
ULTIMATE OWNERS

---

1 The brand-name is emboldened and eye-catching.

2 Distinctive logo will be easily recognisable to youngsters.

3 Emotive word – gives impression that this product has been popular for ever!

4 Emotive appeal playing on the readers' feelings – must have; must be different.

5 Rhetorical questions used as persuasive devices.

6 Picture to give immediate impression of the product and used to give visual impact.

7 Name of the product is eye-catching. The name was chosen to appeal to young people. Use of exclamation mark for emphasis.

8 Pun on the word 'track' – running track and keep up to date with.

9 Alliteration used for effect.

10 Persuasive language.

11 Use of word 'new' encourages people to buy latest product.

12 Incentive offered to buyers.

13 Note that no price is included. This is deemed unnecessary information. It gives the message that the cost is immaterial.

Understanding the grammar and punctuation

Understanding the grammar and punctuation enables children to control the language they use and therefore to write more effectively.

Grammar pointers

Alliteration

Alliteration is a figure of speech in which a sequence of words begins with the same letter or sound. It is frequently used in non-fiction writing to make text more memorable, especially in advertising slogans and titles.

> *Choose the Charnwell Challenge.*

Ambiguity

'Ambiguous' means the meaning is unclear. A sentence that has more than one meaning is ambiguous. Sentences that are badly constructed can sometimes have more than the one intended meaning and while ambiguity may be amusing, it can make your writing difficult to understand.

There are different types of ambiguous sentences:

a) when it is unclear what the pronoun refers to;

> *The teacher shouted at the boy because he was not being nice.*

b) participles can appear to refer to the wrong word in the sentence;

> *Skipping along the road he saw a cow.*

c) words or phrases can appear in the wrong place;

> *He took a photo of the Eiffel Tower flying into Paris.*

d) words can have more than one meaning;

> *Man critical after shooting.*

e) ambiguity can arise from sentence contractions;

> *Police shoot man with knife.*

In advertising, the use of ambiguity is often deliberate to draw attention to the message and to influence the reader.

Puns

A pun is a type of ambiguity. It is a play on words. In advertising, puns are often used to create humour through more than one meaning. They rely on their double meaning to be funny.

> *An advert for a security firm: Been burgled? – Get alarmed!*

Punctuation pointers

Punctuating statements, questions, commands and exclamations

Every sentence begins with a capital letter and ends with a full stop, a question mark or an exclamation mark depending upon whether it is a statement, a question, a command or an exclamation.

- A statement tells you about something. It is the most common type of sentence and it ends with a full stop.
- A question or an interrogative sentence ends with a question mark. Questions often begin with words such as 'who', 'why', 'where', 'how' and 'what' and generally require an answer. Rhetorical questions require no answer. They are often used for effect in persuasive writing and aim to challenge the reader.
- A command sentence that instructs someone to do something often ends with an exclamation mark. An exclamation sentence that uses such words as 'Oh!', 'Well!' and 'Goodness me!' also ends with an exclamation mark. In persuasive writing an exclamation mark is frequently used to denote excitement and wonder.

> *Brilliant!*
> *Amazing!*
> *Wow!*

The children's version of these notes is on page 80 of the Resource book.

Writing features
Persuasive devices

Advertisers use various tactics to persuade us to part with our money. When creating their brochures, leaflets and advertisements, they adopt a variety of techniques to influence the reader.

Language

- Catchy slogans – may focus on a particular brand-name and will promote the product by making powerful statements about it.
  > *Choose the Charnwell Challenge.*
  > *Adike – The Legend.*
- Alliteration – is used to make the message memorable.
  > *Stylish, smooth, strong, sensational.*
- Emotive vocabulary – to evoke an emotional reaction in the reader. For example, words like *tranquil*, *comfortable* and *warm*.
- Vocabulary to target a specific audience – the use of words like *challenge*, *ultimate*, *monster* and *mammoth* will attract a young market.
- Use of key verbs such as 'can' and 'do' – makes the product appear attainable.
- Focusing mainly on generic human participants – addressing the reader directly involves him/her personally.
- Use of the pronoun 'we' – indicates togetherness and makes the reader feel involved.
- Use of puns and wordplay – attracts attention to the message.
  > *Stay on track* – pun on *track*
- Distorting the meaning of words and deliberate misspellings, such as *purrfect* for advertising cat food, are also devices used for immediate reader impact.
- Rhetorical questions – can persuade people to donate money. For example:
  > *Can you sit back and watch children starve?*
  Or to buy goods:
  > *Can you live without it?*
- Mixture of formal and informal language – formal vocabulry is used to make the message appear authoritative and credible, informal vocabulary is used to create a warm, friendly and non-intimidating image.

Fact and opinion

Advertisements will usually be a mixture of fact and opinion. Remind the children that:
- facts can be proved;
- opinions are what someone thinks.

Sometimes in advertising, opinions will be disguised as facts to persuade the reader that a point of view is correct. Phrases that are deliberately ambiguous such as *are believed to be* or *probably the best ... in the world* are used to influence the reader but do not offer genuine proof.

Illustrations

Illustrations are particularly useful in getting the message across. The picture stimulates the first impression of the product and may immediately conjure up a mood or emotion. The best pictures are eye-catching and have sufficient impact to make the reader want to read the advertisement.

The use of colour is an important factor in sending messages to the reader. For example, the use of red implies danger; green may represent an environmentally friendly product and yellow or orange, a healthy promotion.

Exploiting feelings

The advertiser will play upon our human weaknesses and appeal to our hidden desires. He may also appeal to our sense of values. He may exploit our:
- love of flattery;
- desire to have the best for ourselves and our families;
- weakness for self-indulgence;
- desire to be different;
- desire to keep up with technology;
- nose for a bargain or value for money;
- desire to help people or animals in need.

Concessions and incentives

The advertiser may offer concessions and incentives to the readers, in order to attract them to the product. For example, sale bargains, reductions and free gifts.

There are helpful hints for children for writing advertisements and leaflets on page 83 of the Resource book.

Recounts and chronological reports

Recount texts deal with the retelling of events.

In oral form they can range from a child returning home from school and telling his/her parents about the events of the day, to a sports report on radio or television.

In written form recounts may be found in biographies, books detailing historical events, magazine and newspaper reports, or in the form of letters to relatives or friends outlining what has happened in people's lives since they were last in contact.

In schools, children write chronological reports when compiling diaries of the week's events, when writing science experiments and when writing reports on school matches, excursions and field trips.

Recounts generally focus on individual people and the events or happenings they have experienced.

The audience will dictate the style of the recount. For example, a verbal report of a school games match given in assembly will be concise and impersonal, as will a report on a science experiment. A report on a field trip written for a school magazine will include personal details of the writer's experience and he will endeavour to engage the reader's interest by adding amusing or anecdotal incidents.

Whether personal or impersonal in style, a recount is always written chronologically; events unfold sequentially and markers are used to indicate the passing of time.

Recounts

Examples of recounts and chronological reports

Farm Boy by Michael Morpurgo (Pavilion)
Coming Alive: Mary, Queen of Scots by Stewart Ross (Evans)
Samuel Pepys Diary
Ancient Egypt by Amanda Martin, My World series (Two-Can)
Barley Hall – A Day in a Medieval Town House by Charles Knightly (Wayland)
Fishbourne – A Day in a Roman Palace by Tony D Triggs (Wayland)
Race to the Moon by Jan Green (Franklin Watts)

The recount on page 44 is adapted from reports written by Francesca Ghigi and Emily Moore. An illustrated version for children can be found on page 90 of the Resource book.

A recount

A Trip to How Hill – _A Report for the School Magazine_[1]

The day had finally arrived and I was really excited. I couldn't wait. After weeks of planning, I was on my way with the rest of my class, to How Hill, the environmental study centre set in the heart of the Norfolk Broads.[2] We were going to be spending three glorious school free days there![3]

Our first view of the house was amazing; it was a beautiful[4] Edwardian thatched manor house set in its own lovely[4] gardens. I was to share a room with Alice and Laura. The room was quite big and the beds were comfortable[4]. The view from the window was quite magnificent[4] and you could see for miles. You could even see a windmill with the river wending its way round it. No time to stand and stare however, and we quickly[5] unpacked and had lunch.

After lunch we made our way down to the river for dyke dipping. This involved dipping our nets into the dyke to catch a whole variety of creatures. My partner was Alice and we caught an orb cockle, a snail, a blood-worm, a water beetle and a water boatman and our best catch was a caddis-fly nymph. We also found a pond-skater and a mayfly nymph. Eventually, after packing away our equipment, it was time for our nature walk.

We were split into two groups and we visited four different habitats[6]. The first habitat we saw was the grazing marshland. It had squelchy mud and no trees. One of the birds we discovered living there was a marsh-harrier, which eats water voles. The second habitat was the carr woodland[6], which had willow trees, reeds and rather damp ground. In fact it was VERY[7] wet and Claire, our instructor, warned us we might sink. She pulled a gigantic log from the mud;[8] it was as tall as she was and showed just how deep[9] the bog was! The scrape[6] was the third habitat, and this had very shallow water with the top layer of mud scraped off for the wading birds. The final habitat we visited was the dry woodland[6]; the trees there were a lot further apart than in the wet woodland and there were plenty of rotten leaves on the ground. Oak, chestnut and beech trees are all found there. We looked for animals that live under the logs and I found a beetle, a woodlouse, a millipede, a centipede, a worm, a spider and an ant.

Eventually[10] it started to rain so we set off back to the house where we went to the schoolroom and began work on our diaries.

At half past five we had tea. We had fish-fingers and chips and jelly with real orange pieces in.

The day had been long and tiring so we went to bed early – far too exhausted to worry about the How Hill 'ghost'![11]

✶✶✶✶✶✶[12]

I woke early[13], at 6:05 and before anyone else, so I spent a few minutes gazing out of the window and watching the birds swooping to and fro gathering food from the bird table. The morning light over the broads made the water glisten and the scene seem very peaceful. Not for long! The peace was soon shattered[14] as my room-mates woke up and we chattered and clattered our way down to breakfast.

After breakfast[15] we went on a boat trip to Barton Broad. On the way we did a bird survey. We saw lots of birds but my favourite was the great crested grebe because it had really cool hair. We even saw a female carrying her babies on her back. Some snowy white swans[16] came really[17] close to us with their

1	Establishes the audience.
2	Adverbial phrase.
3	Opening paragraph introduces report and answers questions –Where? Why? Who? and When?
4	Use of adjectives to give personal reflections about the venue.
5	Adverb of manner.
6	Specific or technical language used.
7	Capital letters used for emphasis.
8	Adverbial phrase.
9	Adverb of degree.
10	Adverb of time.
11	Added to interest and intrigue the reader.
12	Asterisks used to denote the passing of time.
13	Adverb of time.
14	Sentence starting with the passive.
15	Sentence beginning with adverbial phrase.
16	Sentence starting with a noun phrase.
17	An adverb modifying an adverb.

cygnets following behind so we managed to take some pretty good photos. When we got to Barton Broad we learned why the water is so murky. It happens because the sewage from all the boats and homes and the fertilisers from the nearby farmland enter the water. Then the algae[18] feed on the nitrates[18] and phosphates[18], which helps them grow. The algae make it difficult for any plants or animals to live there because they stop the sunlight coming through. We learned that the food chain[18] at the moment is very unbalanced so we need to help it become balanced again. Despite the murky water and the rather cool breeze out on the open water, it was a memorable excursion and we returned quite exhilarated.

After the boat trip,[19] we went in to the house and warmed up because we were all frozen, and then we had lunch. With some food in our stomachs, we were all raring to go to our next activities, which were thatching and rush-candle making.

We were split into two groups and I did thatching first, which was really fun. We had to thatch part of a roof and when we had finished we did a test to see if our thatch was waterproof. Dr Taylor, our teacher, stood in the house while Sally threw a bucket of water over it to see if it was soundly thatched. Luckily[20] for Dr Taylor, it was! Rush-candle making was rather[21] fun but quite difficult. First of all we collected the rushes and brought them back to peel. Then we took the pith and made a candle. Sadly, mine didn't work out so I had one of Emma's.

When we came back from thatching and rush-candle making, we tried our hand at clay modelling. I didn't know what to make at first, but in the end I made a butterfly and a caterpillar. They worked out quite well and I was pleased with them.

At about 7:15 we strolled down to Toad Hole Cottage, which is a tiny cottage on the estate and which is about 160 years old. It was rather quaint and very interesting, but it was EXTREMELY[22] small and at one time eleven people lived in it! There were only three beds and one cot, so four people had to share a single bed!

By the time we arrived back at the house there was just time for a drink before we rolled thankfully into our beds – just pleased that *we* weren't sharing our beds with three others![23]

******

Our third and final day began with an activity game called 'Hawks and Blackbirds'. It involved blackbirds collecting blackberries from bushes and hawks catching the blackbirds. We, the children, were the blackbirds and the hawks so you can imagine the fun we had.

After this game we went orienteering. Using[24] a compass and bearing we managed to complete four courses, which was pretty impressive. I used the compass twice while Laura marked off and then we swapped roles.

After lunch we went to look at How Hill's exotic water gardens. They were really beautiful with many different kinds of colourful flowers. We were also taken to meet Eric the marsh-man and he demonstrated how to cut the reeds and prepare them for thatching. It was a good opportunity for taking more photos before we had to leave.

Our three days had come to an end and it was time to say good-bye to the beautiful, peaceful surroundings and to the new friends we had made at How Hill. I had learned so many new things – from identifying different species of birds, to thatching roofs, to dyke dipping. It was a thoroughly enjoyable and action-packed trip and I couldn't wait to get back home to tell my parents all about it. Shame that we had to return to school the next day![25]

---

18 Further use of specific and technical language.

19 Signals the passing of time.

20 Starting sentence with an adverb.

21 Adverb modifying adjective.

22 Capital letters used for emphasis.

23 Comment made to amuse the reader and to sum up the section.

24 Sentence starting with a participle.

25 Final paragraph sums up and comments on feelings about the trip.

Understanding the grammar and punctuation

Understanding the grammar and punctuation enables children to control the language they use and therefore to write more effectively.

Grammar pointers

Adjectives

Remind the children that adjectives are describing words. They give us more information about nouns and pronouns and they help to make writing more interesting.

Adjectives are usually found in front of the noun or pronoun and after the words 'a', 'an', 'the' or 'some'. For example:

> *a gigantic log*
>
> *an old cottage*
>
> *the murky water*
>
> *some snowy white swans*

They can also be found after the linking verb in the sentence. For example:

> *The house was amazing.*
>
> *In fact it was very wet.*

Adverbs

Adverbs are used to modify a verb, an adjective or another adverb. For example:

> *We quickly unpacked.* (modifies verb)

The adverb *quickly* tells how we unpacked.

> *Rush-candle making was rather fun.* (modifies adjective)

The adverb *rather* tells us how much fun it was.

> *Some swans came really close.* (modifies adverb)

The adverb *really* tells us how close the swans came.

Adverbs tell us how, when, where, and to what degree something is happening. They answer questions such as:

> Where? – *It was very cold so we went inside.*
>
> When? – *I woke early.*
>
> How? – *She pulled the log from the mud carefully.*
>
> How much? – *I was pretty impressed with my orienteering skills.*

Adverbial phrases perform the same function as adverbs, giving more information about the verbs and the adverbs.

> *set in the heart of the Norfolk Broads*
>
> *she pulled a gigantic log from the mud*

Punctuation pointers

Using capital letters for emphasis

Capital letters may be used to emphasise a particular word and to give prominence to it. This technique can be effective but should be used sparingly.

In the exemplar, the words VERY and EXTREMELY are emphasised with capital letters. Other ways of drawing attention to particular words or phrases are to use italics, to embolden them or to underline them.

Asterisks

Although sentence markers are used to denote the passing of time, in some instances it is useful to include a series of asterisks. These can indicate that a greater amount of time has elapsed. In the exemplar the asterisks mark the arrival of a new day.

> The children's version of these notes is on page 94 of the Resource book.

Writing features
Style and structure

Style

Explain to the children that a report is usually written for someone else to read, so a writer's audience will influence how he/she writes. The style of writing is adapted for different audiences.

Personal

If writing to a friend about a personal experience, such as a school trip or visit or a field trip, the style will be friendly and chatty and may include personal reflections and feelings.

Writing for an unknown reader will require a slightly more formal tone, but will still include details to interest the reader.

In both instances it is the writer's own experiences that influence what he/she writes. Events or happenings are recounted in chronological order but are told as the writer remembers them, so certain incidents may feature more prominently than others.

Impersonal

An impersonal report relies less upon detailed personal experiences and more upon chronologically listed stages or facts. A degree of formality is adopted and technical terms or specific names of people, places or objects may be used.

Structure

Orientation and reorientation

The introduction to a report is used to orientate the reader. It sets the scene and gives any necessary background information to the report. It may also answer the questions 'Who?', 'Where?', 'When?' and 'Why?'
In the exemplar the following are answered:
Who? – The class.
Where? – How Hill Centre.
Why? – Environmental field study.
When? – For three days during school term time.

Recounts often begin:
- I remember when I was ...;
- Last week ...;
- During the summer holidays ...

After the events have been retold, a general summing up or a closing statement is given. This may say something like:
- Overall we had a successful ...;
- When I got back I had to tell ...;

This is often called reorientation.

Sentence starters

Encourage the children to experiment with a variety of sentence beginnings to make their writing more interesting. Sentences may begin with:

- an adverbial phrase such as

    After weeks of planning...

- the use of the passive, such as

    The peace was soon shattered by ...

- a noun phrase followed by a verb, such as

    Some snowy white swans came really close ...

- an adverb, such as

    Luckily for Dr Taylor ...

- a present participle, such as

    Using a compass and bearing ...

They could also consider using a rhetorical question or direct speech to begin a sentence.

> There are helpful hints for children for writing a recount on page 97 of the Resource book.

Non-chronological texts – reports and explanations

Non-chronological writing tackles particular topics in a way that is independent of the passage of time.

This writing may take the form of a report written to inform the reader or a text written to explain a process.

This type of writing requires careful planning: the use of research, cohesive organisation of ideas and secure drafting and editing skills.

The children should be made aware of the fact that when they are researching a subject for topic work and then writing up their notes, they are in fact writing a report on the information they have discovered.

A non-chronological text often begins with a general introduction to orientate the reader, followed by sections on different aspects of the topic. It will conclude with a bibliography to acknowledge sources of information.

Information may be presented in the form of illustrations or diagrams. This is particularly relevant to explanatory texts where labelled or annotated diagrams simplify and clarify ideas.

Other features of non-chronological writing are:

- the use of an impersonal style;
- the use of technical language;
- the use of language to describe and differentiate;
- the sustained use of the present tense;
- the use of the passive voice;
- the use of linking words and phrases.

Non-chronological writing in school will often be linked to other curriculum areas and this type of writing will be extended outside the literacy hour.

Non-chronological reports

Examples of non-chronological texts

Natural Disasters by James Brian (Rigby Magic Bean 1993)
My Tudor Home by Karen Bryant-Mole (Franklin Watts 1995)
Coastline Journey by Christine Butterworth (Ginn All Aboard 1998)
The Victorians in Britain by Peter Chrisp (Franklin Watts 1999)
Hindu by Anita Ganeri (Franklin Watts 1997)
Minibeast Pets, Slugs and Snails by Theresa Greenaway (Wayland 1999)
Wasps, Stings and Wriggly Things by Martin Jenkins (Walker 1996)
Quakes, Floods and other Disasters by Fred Martin (Heinemann Literacy World 1994)
Mountains by Steve Parker (Franklin Watts 1997)
Christianity by Sue Penney (Heinemann 1997)
The Earth in Space by Peter Riley (Ginn All Aboard 1998)
A family from Japan by Simon Scoones (Wayland 1997)

The children's illustrated version of the report is on page 104 of the Resource book.

A non-chronological text -1

France

France lies in the west of Europe[1]. It is the largest country in Europe and in area is about twice the size of Britain. It is less crowded, however, since its population is only about half that of Britain. France has borders with eight different countries and coastlines on the Atlantic Ocean, the Mediterranean Sea and the English Channel. It is linked to the UK by the Channel Tunnel. France is rich in culture and steeped in history. It is a land of varying geographical features:[2] from rolling pasture-land to deep forests; to picturesque towns and villages;[3] to high snow-capped mountains. It is also one of the world's leading agricultural and industrial nations. Thousands of tourists from all over the world visit France for its beautiful countryside, its sandy beaches, its winter sports and, of course, to explore its capital, Paris.[4]

Paris[4] is one of the most beautiful cities in the world[5]. It is France's largest city and its main cultural and business centre. It is also one of the leading fashion centres of the world. Each spring, designers from all over the world come to view the work of famous fashion houses and the Paris collections are copied all over the world. Paris's world-famous sights include the Eiffel Tower, the Champs Elysées and Montmartre. The white church of the Sacré Coeur stands on a hill overlooking the district of Montmartre. This was once the haunt of famous artists such as Toulouse-Lautrec, Renoir and Picasso, and today you can still see artists at work there. The cathedral of Notre Dame stands on an island in the River Seine. This island is called the Ile de la Cité and is the oldest part of Paris. It is the area where the city was founded about 2,000 years ago by the Romans.[6]

For about 500 years, France was part of the Roman Empire and then, after the fall of the Roman Empire, it was conquered by a Germanic tribe called the Franks (France takes its name from the Franks)[7]. Eventually it became a number of different countries. Large areas were once ruled by England, but in the 16th century the English were driven out, leaving it as one country ruled by a king. In 1789 there was a revolution when the poor people of France rebelled against the monarchy. It began with the capture of the Bastille prison in Paris on 14 July. Today, Bastille Day is a national holiday with parties, processions and fireworks. After the revolution, the monarchy was replaced by a government chosen by the people, and the country became a republic (France's full name is The Republic of France).[7]

France stretches 1,000 kilometres from north to south and from east to west and is hexagonal in shape. The countryside varies greatly from fertile farmland to the snow-capped peaks of the Pyrenees and the Alps mountain ranges. Between these two mountain ranges, the southern coastline runs alongside the Mediterranean Sea and boasts lovely sandy beaches popular with tourists seeking sun and sea. The northern coastline is more rugged and faces the stormy Atlantic Ocean. Inland France is mainly meadows and woodland. France has more farmland than any other country in Europe;[8] in fact just over half the land is farmland, and wheat, barley, grapes and apples are the main crops.

1 The opening sentence of the introductory paragraph is written to orientate the reader. This paragraph gives information on France in general terms.

2 Use of a colon to introduce a list.

3 Semicolons are used to separate items in a list when the items are long.

4 The repetition of 'Paris' links the first and second paragraphs.

5 The opening sentence of the paragraph is a topic sentence introducing the main idea of the paragraph – Paris.

6 Closing sentence in paragraph links to the next paragraph, ie the history of France.

7 Brackets used to give extra information.

8 Use of a semicolon.

France has contrasts in climate[9]. "The north west and south west usually have cool summers and mild winters with frequent rain while the mountainous regions in the east have warm summers and cold winters with lots of snow. The south coast has little rain, warm winters and hot dry summers."*[10] The climate in the north and central areas is suited to cereal crops and livestock while the sunny south is ideal for fruit growing. Huge fields of sunflowers are grown in southern France and the seeds are used to make sunflower oil. Many regions and towns in France are known throughout the world for their wine and cheese:[11] the country produces about a quarter of the world's wine and over 400 varieties of cheese.

The varying climate combined with the physical features of the countryside dictates where most people live. Many live in the south of France due to the milder climate, while very few live in the mountain regions. Only about a quarter of the people live in the countryside;[12] the rest live in towns and cities. As a result the French countryside is relatively spacious and uncrowded. Most of the larger towns and cities are located near the coast or along the Rhone, the Seine, the Loire or the Garonne, France's four main rivers. They are centres of trade, industry and tourism. "There are many different types of homes in France. In villages most people live in houses with gardens but three-quarters of the French population live in towns and cities where almost everyone lives in apartments."**

Family life is very important to the French and the average family spends a lot of time together[13]. At weekends the whole family will often go out for the day or enjoy sporting activities together. The French love their food and like to eat it very fresh so, as well as visiting supermarkets and hypermarkets, they will buy food daily at local shops or the markets. They will also often go out to eat at local restaurants and enjoy delicacies such as:[14] escargots (snails)[15], frogs' legs, paté and crepes (pancakes)[15]. When they eat at home, meals consist of numerous courses and can last for several hours. Most families, sometimes including the children, drink wine with their meals. Some areas of France are famous for particular food dishes: the area around Marseilles is famous for its fish soup;[16] Normandy for its apple tarts. France is well known for its delicious cooking!

France is a land of many contrasts. It is a prosperous country and plays a key role in European and world affairs. It works closely with other European countries to make a wealthier Europe for all.[17]

* Fisher, Teresa. *France,* Country Insights series (Wayland, 1996)[18]
** ibid[19]

Bibliography[20]

Bibbings, Susan and Gillian, Wrobel. *France*, Looking at Lands series (Macdonald Educational, 1980)
Boast, Clare. *France*, Step into series (Heinemann, 1997)
Fisher, Teresa. *France*, Country Insights series (Wayland, 1996)
Ganeri, Anita. *France and the French*, Focus on series (Gloucester Press, 1992)
Somerville, Louisa. *First Book of France* (Usborne, 1989)
Thompson, Kenneth. *About France* (Cassell, 1990)

9   Topic sentence to begin paragraph on climate. Links with previous paragraph and gives the main ideas followed by examples.

10 The quote is asterisked and the source is indicated at the end of the text.

11 Use of a colon. The second statement explains the first.

12 A semicolon is used to link two simple sentences.

13 A topic sentence based on opinion/belief.

14 A colon is used to introduce list.

15 Brackets are used to give extra information – in this case, the English translation.

16 A semicolon is used to contrast two ideas when the same verb applies to both.

17 A brief conclusion.

18 Gives the source of the quote.

19 This means 'in the same place', ie a quote taken from the same source.

20 A bibliography to acknowledge sources of information.

A non-chronological text – 2

How we hear

All sounds are sets of vibrations; they are tiny, intense waves travelling through the air. The ear is the part of the body[1] that collects the sound, funnels it through the ear-hole to the middle ear, and on to the inner ear where a signal is sent to the brain.

The ear is made up of three parts: the outer ear, the middle ear and the inner ear.

The outer ear is the part that can be seen. It funnels sound into the ear canal towards the _eardrum_[2]. The sound hits the eardrum and makes it vibrate. The sound vibrations are passed[3] from the eardrum along two small bones called the _hammer_[2] and the _anvil_[2] and then along a group of tiny bones called the _stirrup_[2]. These bones are part of the middle ear.

The bones of the middle ear send[4] the sound waves through to the inner ear where there is a sheet of very thin skin called the _oval window_[2], which is stretched over an opening. The sound is passed along to this membrane and then into a fluid filled tube, which looks rather like a snail and is called the _cochlea_[2]. When the sound waves pass through tiny hairs in the cochlea it sends messages to the brain and the brain interprets the messages.

This is how we hear.[5]

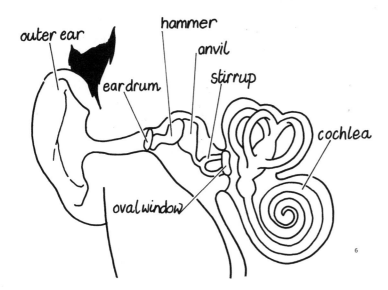

outer ear · hammer · anvil · stirrup · eardrum · cochlea · oval window

Bibliography[7]

Davies, Nick. _How Our Bodies Work_, Factfinders series (BBC, 1990)
Taylor, Barbara. _About Your Body_, Everyday Science series (Wayland, 1994)

The opening paragraph sets out the function of the ear in general terms. Later paragraphs give more specific information.

1 Use of impersonal language – 'the ear' rather than 'my/your ear'.

2 The correct vocabulary is used.

3 The use of the agentless passive.

4 The active voice is used.

5 The concluding paragraph is simply one sentence.

6 A labelled diagram helps simplify and clarify information.

7 A bibliography acknowledges sources of information.

Understanding the grammar and punctuation

Understanding the grammar and punctuation

Understanding the grammar and punctuation enables children to control their language and therefore to write more effectively.

Grammar pointers

Paragraphs

A paragraph is a collection of sentences that explore one idea. All sentences written in a paragraph should relate to the main idea of that paragraph.

A paragraph is variable in length; it may be only a couple of sentences long or ten or more.

The topic sentence is the main idea for the whole paragraph. It is often the opening sentence.

* It may give the central idea the writer is trying to get across to the reader, followed by an example.

  France has contrasts in climate. The north west and south west usually have ...

* It may give the beliefs or opinions of the writer.

  Family life is very important to the French and the average family spends a lot of time together. At weekends...

* It may say what the writer is describing, followed by more detailed description.

  Paris is one of the most beautiful cities in the world. It is France's largest city ...

It is also possible to have the topic sentence as a concluding sentence.

Linking paragraphs

In non-chronological writing, paragraphs often introduce new aspects of the topic. They are separated by either leaving a line between them or indenting the start of each paragraph. It is important, however, in all writing that paragraphs link with one another in a coherent way.

To establish the relationship between paragraphs and to indicate links, new paragraphs can be introduced with appropriate connectives. These could be:

* logical connecters, for example

  Although, However, Nevertheless

* connecting phrases, for example

  For instance, On the other hand

* adverbs of time, for example

  Meanwhile, Consequently, Eventually

* repetition of words or phrases, for example

  ...to explore its capital, Paris. Paris is one of the ...

The passive

Sentences can be active or passive. The sentence is said to be active when the subject does the action.

  The bones of the middle ear (the subject) send the sound waves through to the inner ear.

The sentence is said to be passive when the action of the verb is done to the subject.

  The sound waves (the subject) are sent by the bones of the middle ear through to the inner ear.

In this case 'the bones of the middle ear' act as the agent doing the action.

The passive is constructed by adding the past participle of the verb to the appropriate form of the verb 'to be'.

  The sound is passed along the membrane to...

In this sentence the agent is concealed.

An agentless passive is used when it is unnecessary to know who or what is doing the action. In non-chronological texts the passive form is often chosen because it makes the writing impersonal.

Understanding the grammar and punctuation

Punctuation pointers

Colons and semicolons can help to organise and structure writing.

Colons

They are used:

- to introduce a list, for example

    They will also often go out to eat at local restaurants and enjoy delicacies such as: escargots, frogs' legs, paté and crepes.

- to separate two statements when the second explains the first

    Many regions and towns in France are known throughout the world for their wine and cheese: the country produces about a quarter of the world's wine and over 400 varieties of cheese.

- to introduce direct speech or quotations.

Semicolons

The semicolon is a useful punctuation mark. It is stronger than the comma but not as strong as a full stop.

Semicolons are used:

- to separate items in a complicated list

    It is a land of varying geographical features: from rolling pasture-land to deep forests; to picturesque towns and villages; to high snow-capped mountains.

- instead of a conjunction to link simple sentences

    Only about a quarter of the people live in the countryside; the rest live in towns and cities.

- to contrast two ideas when the same verb is applied to both

    The area around Marseilles is famous for its fish soup; Normandy for its apple tarts.

> The children's version of these notes is on page 108 of the Resource book.

Writing features
Gathering information and acknowledging sources

Gathering information

Explain to the children that research just means finding out about things and there are various ways of doing this:

- finding reference books;
- searching CD-Roms;
- searching the Internet.

Although they should be familiar with accessing information from their computer and from a library, children need to be reminded how to find their way around these sources of information.

When researching information from books the children should be aware of the following:

- the contents page – this lists the chapters, sections or units and may be the first source of retrieving information;
- the index – this is a list in alphabetical order of all the main topics mentioned in the book with relevant page numbers;
- the glossary – this is a dictionary of any special or technical words used in the book;
- the bibliography – as well as listing books referred to by the author, it will often give further reading material on the same subject. This is invaluable to the researcher.

When gathering information, the children should make notes (see Unit 2) from each source of information that has a common theme, and arrange these notes under suitable headings. These can then be used as paragraph plans for their writing.

Acknowledging sources

It is important that children can identify ways in which authors record and acknowledge their sources and that they, too, are able to acknowledge sources in their own writing.

Using quotes

Explain to the children that quotes are words taken directly from a source of information and then used in the author's own writing. The writer cannot copy someone else's work without acknowledging it. To do this he/she uses quotation marks.

> *"The north west and south west usually have cool summers and mild winters with frequent rain while the mountainous regions in the east have warm summers and cold winters with lots of snow."**

The writer then numbers or asterisks the quote and at the end of the text he/she states where the words came from.

> **Fisher, Teresa. Country Insights France (Wayland, 1996)*

If two quotes are from the same source, the abbreviation 'ibid' is used, which means 'in the same place'.

The bibliography

Explain to the children that the bibliography should be arranged in alphabetical order according to the surname of the author; then the title of the book should be written, followed by the publisher and the date of publication. If CD-Roms and Internet sites are used, these should also be recorded in the bibliography.

There are helpful hints for children for writing a non-chronological report on page 111 of the Resource book.

Journalistic writing

'The media' refers to any things that convey information from one person to another. When information is conveyed to a great number of people at the same time it is referred to as 'mass media'. The most obvious examples are television, radio, the Internet and newspapers.

There are a number of types of newspaper and although all newspapers have access to the same information, they choose to interpret it in many different ways. The type of newspaper will affect the audience and therefore its content, language and style.

A local newspaper contains some national and international news, but focuses on fairly local news topics in detail. It is usually based round a town, a city or a group of villages. Examples are 'The Biggleswade Chronicle' and 'The Bristol Evening News'.

A regional paper contains some national and international news, but focuses on news relating to a specific area of the country. Examples are 'The Eastern Daily Press' and 'The Bedfordshire Times'.

A national newspaper covers news across the whole country together with international news. Examples are 'The Daily Express' and 'The Guardian'.

A tabloid is a newspaper that covers all national and international news but aims for popular appeal and often contains a certain amount of gossipy news. It might sensationalise or exaggerate news items. Examples are 'The News of the World' and 'The Sun'.

A broadsheet is the largest type of newspaper. It covers all national and international news, often in a serious or formal way. In general it keeps to the established facts and respects the feelings of those concerned, covering only personal details that are of public interest. Examples are 'The Times' and 'The Observer'.

Although newspapers carry a variety of articles, they all have typical features:
*   headlines – to catch the reader's eye and to encourage them to read the story;
*   a topic sentence – usually the first sentence of the report to explain what the story is about;
*   short paragraphs – to enable the reader to locate information quickly;
*   columns – to make the article easier to read;
*   use of different type faces – to add interest and enhance the design;
*   photographs – to add interest and authenticity to the story;
*   quotations – to give an air of truth or reality to the story.

The children may have had experience of writing editorials: putting forward one point of view in a report and using a persuasive style. In this unit they will learn how to develop a journalistic style through considering:
*   balanced and biased reporting;
*   what is of public interest in events;
*   interest of the reader;
*   selection and presentation of information.

Journalistic writing

Newspapers – local, regional, national, tabloids and broadsheets.
Greek Gazette by Paul Dowswell, Newspaper History series (Usborne, 1997)
The Roman News by Philip Gates and Ghislaine Lawrence (Walker Books 1994.)
Others in the series cover Egyptians, Aztecs, Vikings, Greeks and the Stone Age.

The children's versions of the following newspaper reports are on pages 118 and 119 of the Resource book.

The Chronicle

BURGLED FARMER SENT TO JAIL[1]

Hero[2]

Farmer John Smith was being hailed as a hero yesterday as he left court after being convicted of attempted murder and given a 10-year jail sentence.[3]

Crowds outside the courtroom jeered at officials as they led Mr. Smith to the waiting police van, and clearly demonstrated their support for the Cambridgeshire farmer.

John Smith, 57, from Little Dopping, was defending[4] his home from intruders last September, when he shot and wounded 17-year-old James Brown, an unemployed labourer of no fixed address.[5]

Confusion

It was 1.30 on the morning of the 22nd September when Mr. Smith, a well-respected member of the local community[6], was woken by the sound of breaking glass and voices beneath his bedroom window.

After reassuring his wife[7], and taking up a shotgun which he kept in the house for shooting foxes and rabbits on his farm, Mr. Smith made his way downstairs to confront the intruders. In the ensuing confusion and the darkness, a gunshot was fired and Brown lay seriously wounded.[8]

Three other members of Brown's gang fled the scene but were later apprehended.

Mr. Smith immediately informed the police of the incident and was promptly arrested and charged with the attempted murder of Brown.

Long line of burglaries

It appears that this break-in was the last in a series of similar incidents in Little Dopping. There had been a spate of burglaries and thefts in the local area and it emerged that Mr. Smith himself had been the victim[9] of eight burglaries in the past eighteen months.

An Englishman's castle

A neighbour of Mr. Smith is quoted as saying: 'We are fed up to the teeth with the number of break-ins in this neighbourhood. We have reported all these incidents to the police but until now, no one has ever been caught or charged with these crimes. It's about time something was done. We are furious that John has been jailed. He was simply defending his home and family and acting in self-defence against those yobs. After all, an Englishman's home is his castle, isn't it?'[10]

Since the incident, James Brown has made a full recovery.

Lawyers for Mr. Smith stated yesterday that the case will definitely go to appeal.[11]

---

1. Eye-catching headline written in bold letters. Wording identifies slant of article – implies injustice.

2. Subheadings. Single word or phrase to sum up message of paragraph. Emotive language used to give the impression that Smith has been wrongly convicted.

3. Topic sentence tells why the story is written. Following sentences give details of what, why, where, when, who and how.

4. Use of the word 'defending' shows bias towards Mr. Smith.

5. Details of James Brown – negative vocabulary used to give poor impression.

6. Positive vocabulary – favourable impression given of Mr. Smith.

7. Emphasises good character – image of a family man.

8. Facts are confused.

9. Use of word 'victim' applied to Smith begs the question, 'Who was the victim?'

10. Long quote from a supporter of Mr. Smith. No quote given from the other side – Brown's family or friends.

11. Closing paragraph states what point the story has reached.

The Paxton Press

FARMER JAILED FOR SHOOTING[1]

A Cambridgeshire farmer was jailed for ten years yesterday after being found guilty of attempted murder.[2]

Break-in[3]

John Smith, 57, from Little Dopping, disturbed a gang of youths breaking into[4] his home last September. It was 1.30 on the morning of 22nd September when John Smith was woken by the sound of breaking glass and voices beneath his bedroom window. After arming himself with a shotgun, he made his way downstairs where he confronted the intruders.[5] According to police, the youngsters fled as Smith began shouting and firing his shotgun. James Brown, a 17-year-old labourer[6], was seriously wounded in the incident.

Spate of burglaries

The break-in was the last in a long series of similar incidents in the area. There had been a spate of burglaries and thefts and Smith had reported several break-ins at his home in the previoius 18 months.

Cold-blooded attack

The prosecution claimed that Smith, angry and intent on revenge, had lain in wait for the intruders to enter

John Smith is taken away.

his home, whereupon he had deliberately taken a loaded shotgun and cold-bloodedly fired at the youth.[7]

Self-defence

Smith's defence lawyers refuted the claim saying that he was simply trying to defend himself, his family and his home. He kept a loaded shotgun in the house because he was having trouble with foxes on his land. On the night in question Smith was frightened by his assailants and in the confusion a shot was fired.[8]

A police spokesman said, 'While we have every sympathy for Mr. Smith, who has suffered considerably at the hands of these youths and who has obviously been frustrated by their evading detention, people cannot just take the law into their own hands. Mr. Smith's sentence must serve as a warning to all those who think they can do so.'[9]

Smith's lawyers confirmed yesterday that he would appeal.[10]

1 Headline is simply informative.

2 Opening paragraph states facts.

3 Subheadings are balanced and give clear indications of paragraph topics.

4 Example of the many prepositions used in the report.

5 Note the subordinate clauses in this sentence.

6 A main clause with an embedded adjectival phrase.

7 This paragraph gives one side of the issue.

8 Gives the other side of the issue.

9 Quote from the police spokesman is balanced and puts forward both views. Quotation marks used.

10 Closing statement gives the point the story has reached at the time of writing. Compare with the language of the closing paragraph in 'The Chronicle'.

Understanding the grammar and punctuation

Understanding the grammar and punctuation enables children to control their language and therefore to write more effectively.

Grammar pointers

Clauses

A clause is a group of words that contains a verb and forms part of a sentence. When two simple sentences are joined by the conjunctions 'and' or 'but' this is called a 'compound sentence'. The two original sentences are then called the 'clauses' of the new sentence.

> *The other members of Brown's gang fled the scene. They were later apprehended.*

Compound sentence:

> *The other members of Brown's gang fled the scene but they were later apprehended.*

A sentence may contain one main clause and other clauses (subordinate clauses). For example:

> *Mr. Smith was a well-respected farmer* (main) *who lived in Cambridgeshire* (subordinate).

Or it may have more than one main clause. For example:

> *Mr. Smith went downstairs* (main) *and he was confronted by the intruders* (main).

Remind the children that a main clause is the only type of clause that can stand as a sentence. A subordinate clause does not make sense on its own.

Sometimes the main clause makes a 'sandwich' round another clause.

> *The police, who were called to the house, arrested Mr. Smith.*

The clause in the middle is called the 'embedded clause' and is enclosed by commas.

Phrases

A phrase is a group of words that makes sense but cannot stand alone as a sentence. A phrase may be missing a verb or a subject to make it complete. Phrases are added to sentences for specific purposes.

An adjectival phrase enhances the description of something or someone.

> *James Brown, <u>a 17-year-old labourer</u>, was seriously wounded.*

An adverbial phrase enhances the description of how, when or where something happens or is done.

> *He kept his gun for shooting rabbits <u>on his farm</u>.*

In newspaper reports, phrases are sometimes used as subheadings. They highlight the important points in paragraphs.

> *Long line of burglaries*
> *An Englishman's castle*

A phrase is often introduced by a preposition.

> *in the local area, on his farm*

Prepositions

Prepositions are linking words that show the relationship between two parts of a sentence. For example:

> *about, on, in, under, through, up, for, below, along, before, off.*

They should be placed between the words they link.

> *The intruders broke <u>into</u> his home.*

> *He heard the sound <u>of</u> breaking glass <u>beneath</u> his bedroom window.*

Punctuation pointers

Quotation marks

Quotation marks are used in newspaper reports to signify the actual words spoken by eye-witnesses or other interviewees.

> *A neighbour of Mr. Smith is quoted as saying: "We are fed up to the teeth with the number of break-ins in the neighbourhood."*

The quotation marks are sometimes preceded by a colon. They consist of a set of single (' ') or double (" ") inverted commas.

Quotation marks are also sometimes used to enclose titles of newspapers, books, plays, television programmes and so on.

> *'The Sunday Times' is a broadsheet but 'The Sun' is a tabloid.*

> The children's version of these notes is on page 120 of the Resource book.

Writing features

Balance and bias

Newspaper reports are written to inform the reader and in the main should give a balanced, unbiased account of the news.

In a balanced report, the writer presents the facts either with no comment at all or with equal weight given to both sides of an issue. In the exemplar, the journalist on 'The Paxton Press' is writing a balanced report. He is reporting the facts, and both sides of the issue are represented.

Bias is putting across an unfair or unbalanced opinion. In a biased report it is clear which side the writer is on since he or she ignores one side of an issue and only presents his or her interpretation of events. The writer does not present the full facts to enable the reader to make up his or her own mind. In the exemplar, the reporter on 'The Chronicle' is biased in favour of Mr. Smith, the farmer. By using emotive language, the writer gives us the impression that Mr. Smith is an innocent victim of crime. Even the sub-headings give the impression that he has been wronged.

Newspaper reports should leave the readers feeling that they understand exactly what has happened.

Headlines

Headlines are intended to attract the reader's attention to a story. They feature the following:
- short punchy sentences;
- emphasis on the main point of the story;
- large bold type;
- the present tense;
- the active voice.

Different newspapers use different styles of headlines. These may:
- be informative – 'Farmer Jailed For Shooting';
- use alliteration – 'Have-A-Go Hero Hauled In';
- be balanced round a preposition – '10 Years For Have-A-Go Hero';
- use puns – 'Chicken Farmer Falls Foul of the Law';
- use exclamations – 'Ridiculous!';
- using slang – 'Porridge for Poultry Farmer';
- be sensational – 'Farmer Opens Fire on Children!'

The inverted pyramid

When writing newspaper articles, journalists will use what is called 'The Inverted Pyramid'. This is so called because the most important or weightier items in a story appear first in the article. These will include the five 'Ws' and one 'How':
- who – names the subject of the story. It can be a person, a group, a building, an institution or a concept;
- what – tells the action that takes place;
- when – tells the time the action is happening;
- why – explains the action;
- where – the place where the action is happening;
- how – describes the manner of the action.

The second paragraph will add details to the story and subsequent paragraphs will provide background information and less important details.

Articles are written in this way because they are easy to read and easy to edit. The essentials of the story will still appear should the story need to be cut by the newspaper editor.

> There are helpful hints for children for writing a newspaper report on page 123 of the Resource book.

Discursive texts

Discursive texts look at two or more points of view about an issue. They discuss the pros and cons of each point of view and examine the evidence for these before reaching a conclusion or leaving the readers to make their own decisions about the subject.

When writing discussion texts, it is important to write a balanced report; those that are heavily biased in one direction are really persuasive rather than discursive. The writer should summarise fairly the competing views and analyse the strengths and weaknesses of different positions. He or she should reinforce arguments with supporting evidence using statistics, quotations from official sources and personal testimonies.

Although discursive texts are similar to argumentative ones in that the writer argues an issue, the writer of an argumentative text wants the reader to believe his or her opinions, so will construct a believable argument for one side only of an issue and will highlight flaws in the opposing argument. He or she may appeal directly to people's emotions. In discursive texts, the writer argues equally both sides of an issue without diverting the reader with emotive language. He or she will not necessarily take a particular stance.

Discursive writing often features controversial issues such as human or animal rights or environmental issues. When asking children to write discursively, however, issues that affect them personally or which they can easily relate to, such as 'Should schools hold sports days?', make equally suitable subjects. Many issues can indeed be drawn from topics in other curriculum areas.

Discursive texts

Examples of discursive texts

Animal Rights by Anita Ganeri, What's the Big Idea? series (Hodder, 1997)
The Mystery of Crop Circles by Alexandra Parsons, Can Science Solve? series (Heinemann, 1999)
Vegetarianism by Samantha Calvert, We're Talking About series (Wayland, 1997)
Why do People Take Drugs by Judith Hemming, Let's Talk About series (Gloucester Press, 1995)
Big Issues by Brian Moses, Literacy World series (Heinemann, 1999)

The children's illustrated version of the discursive text is on page 130 of the Resource book.

Discursive texts

Should animals be used for the purpose of medical research?

Every year over three million animals are used for experimentation purposes in British laboratories. Scientists experiment on these animals for purposes of medical research – they are used in the quest to find cures for illnesses and diseases. Experimentation on living animals is called 'vivisection' and thousands of creatures including mice, rats, monkeys, cats and dogs are infected with diseases, are operated on or die at the hands of scientists.[1]

People have strong views as to whether vivisection is justified. Those who support experimentation on animals believe history has proved that medical advances have been made because of vivisection, and that it is perfectly acceptable to sacrifice the lives of animals in order to save human lives. In contrast[2], those against vivisection argue that it is morally wrong to experiment on animals solely for the benefit of humans, and that all animals should have equal rights. Furthermore[3], they question medical evidence produced by the scientists.[4]

Supporters of vivisection use a number of arguments to reinforce their views, the most persuasive being that experiments on animals are essential in the search for new drugs. Diseases that were fatal in past times have now been virtually wiped out because of vaccines[5] originally tested on animals. Vaccines[5] for polio, tetanus and smallpox were all developed from animal experimentation. Animals themselves have also benefited since vaccines for distemper in dogs and enteritis in cats were first tested on animals.[6]

In addition[7], scientists study the effect of drugs on animals in order to develop medicines for people with long-term conditions[8] such as diabetes and asthma. While no cure has yet been found for these diseases[8], with ongoing research into drugs, life for the sufferers can be made easier and freer from debilitating symptoms.[9]

It is fair to say[10] that scientists are concerned with the wellbeing of laboratory animals and there are strict controls. Wherever possible the use of animals is replaced by other methods of research, and if this is not possible, the number of animals used is kept to an absolute minimum. Tests are also carried out in such a way to cause the least amount of stress.[9]

Computer research plays a significant role in modern research but it is only after testing drugs on animals that doctors are confident in testing them on humans. Thus, animal experimenters claim that their research is vital to further advance medical skills[11].

Those opposed to vivisection claim that, apart from the suffering they cause, animal experiments produce results that are unreliable. They state that because animals do not get the same illnesses as humans, and because their bodies work in different ways from ours, research gives information only about animals and not humans. Animals react to drugs differently from humans. For example[12], drugs like aspirin and paracetamol are highly poisonous to cats, and penicillin kills guinea pigs. Drugs such as thalidomide (a drug used to prevent morning sickness in pregnant women and which caused terrible deformities in the unborn child) have been passed as 'safe' in

1. Opening paragraph to orientate the reader. Definition of vivisection helps reader fully understand topic for discussion.

2. Connective used to introduce opposition of idea.

3. Connective used to add idea.

4. Second paragraph (not underlined) gives a preview of main argument.

5. Repetition of the word 'vaccine' links sentences.

6. Third paragraph (not underlined) is used to support argument for vivisection.

7. Connective used to add idea.

8. Repetition to link sentences, but word is replaced by another of similar meaning.

9. Fourth and fifth paragraphs – again used to support argument.

10. Connective of opinion.

11. Closing argument in favour of vivisection. Use of emotive word – 'vital'.

12. Connective to give example.

animal tests and yet when given to humans have caused dangerous side effects.[13] It is only when drugs have been used in trials on humans that they can be declared truly safe or unsafe.[14]

The single most important aspect of healthcare has been the prevention of disease. At the time of vaccine development, fewer lives were being lost to tuberculosis, smallpox and typhoid because of social improvements, such as better food, better living conditions, clean water and proper sewerage systems. So it is argued[15] that even without the vaccines, many of these diseases would have been eradicated.[16]

Likewise, in today's world, the main causes of death in many countries are poverty-linked diseases often associated with dirty water. Opponents to animal experimentation believe that although these diseases can be _treated_[17] with vaccines and medicines, it is more important to _prevent_[17] them in the first place by improving living conditions. Thus the need for medication would be reduced.[16]

Anti-vivisectionists lobby for humane research. They want to see cures for diseases as much as anyone else but they believe that cruelty to animals in laboratories is not the way to go about it. They maintain that by using methods such as chemical analysis, test tube experiments and computer technology and by using human volunteers and concentrating on human data, significant medical progress will continue to be made.[18]

In conclusion[19], it has been established that research on animals has advanced our knowledge and understanding of diseases and cures and has made possible many life-saving operations including kidney and heart transplants.[20] People's lives have been enriched by using drugs to control and alleviate symptoms of illnesses and vast numbers of people have benefited from modern anaesthetics, all of which have developed through experimentation on animals. For these reasons[21] pro-vivisectionists believe that experiments on animals are entirely justified.[22]

On the other hand[23], it has been proved that animal testing can be unreliable and even dangerous. The most important factor in the search for improved health is still disease prevention and the fight against social problems and poverty. Above all, people who oppose animal experiments believe that it is cruel and unjust to inflict pain and death[24] on animals in laboratories.[22]

13 Backing up claims with facts and specific evidence.

14 First paragraph (not underlined) used to refute argument.

15 Connective to indicate opposing ideas.

16 Second and third paragraphs (not underlined) stating opposing views.

17 Italics used for emphasis.

18 Final paragraph (not underlined) giving opposing views.

19 Connective used to summarise.

20 Specific examples used as evidence to support argument.

21 Connective used for reason.

22 Concluding paragraphs (not underlined) sum up both sides of the argument.

23 Connective used to give opposing summary.

24 Use of emotive language.

Understanding the grammar and punctuation

Understanding the grammar and punctuation enables children to control their language and therefore to write more effectively.

Grammar pointers

Connectives

It is important to link paragraphs together in a way that makes them flow smoothly and logically. Connectives are used to give a natural, cohesive feel to writing and to help the audience move from one point to the next.

In discursive texts, connectives have a variety of functions. They may:

- give a sense of time – *first, secondly, once, eventually, ultimately, previously, meanwhile, sometimes, soon;*
- add an idea – *as well as, moreover, furthermore, in addition, similarly, also;*
- give an opposing idea – *but, however, on the other hand, in contrast, although;*
- give examples – *for instance, for example, as follows;*
- give cause or reason – *for, because, since, nevertheless, thus, therefore, consequently, as a result of;*
- highlight or emphasise ideas – *in particular, as far as I am concerned, with regard to;*
- give summary or conclusion – *therefore, to conclude, in short, in general, in summy.*

Ideas can also be linked by repetition. This does not necessarily mean repeating the same word; the word can be repeated in different forms or may be replaced with one of a similar meaning.

> **Drugs** *like aspirin and paracetamol are highly poisonous to cats and penicillin kills guinea pigs.* **Drugs** *such as thalidomide ...*

> *...for people with* **long-term conditions** *such as diabetes and asthma. While no cure has yet been found for these* **diseases** *...*

Punctuation pointers

How punctuation can alter meaning

Punctuation marks are used to clarify meaning. It is important to use them correctly as the meaning of a sentence can change according to the punctuation marks used.

For example – strategic comma placing:

> *Animal experimenters claim anti-vivisectionists do not advance medical research.*

> *Animal experimenters, claim anti-vivisectionists, do not advance medical research.*

For example – use of speech marks:

> *"Dr. Jones," said the Prime Minister, "is involved in valuable medical research."*

> *Dr. Jones said the Prime Minister is involved in valuable medical research.*

The children's version of these notes is on page 132 of the Resource book.

Writing features
Structuring arguments

When writing discursive texts, the following structure is often used.

The first paragraph is an opening statement. It introduces the subject under discussion and may include some background or some history of the argument.

The second paragraph should give a preview of the main argument, stating clearly the two sides of the issue.

The next two or three paragraphs are used to make points to support the issue. Each paragraph should deal with one idea only, and must be backed up with evidence.

Arguments may be supported in the following ways:

* with facts and statistics;
* by quoting official sources or the opinions of important people;
* by using case studies or giving specific examples;
* by using the writer's own experiences and opinions;
* by appealing to the audience's emotions.

In putting forward one side of the issue, the writer may pre-empt counter arguments using statements such as, 'It has been argued that …'

Subsequent paragraphs are used to present points of view that refute the argument. Each paragraph should deal with separate counter issues, and evidence to reinforce ideas should be supplied.

In writing discursive texts, the author should aim to use appropriate language:

* to connect his ideas logically;
* to make his points clearly and precisely;
* to persuade his audience;
* to show cause and effect.

Language that is too emotive, however, is to be avoided and the points should be argued sensibly, coherently and as convincingly as possible. It is also important to avoid:

* exaggeration – such as 'Millions of animals are needlessly slaughtered in laboratories.';
* illogical argument – such as 'Vaccines do not help eradicate disease because clean water is the solution.';
* abusive argument – such as 'Only stupid people believe that animals should be used for experimentation.';
* statements or statistics that can be challenged – such as 'Better social conditions wiped out the diseases of smallpox, typhoid and tuberculosis.'

The final paragraph sums up both sides of the argument and ends with a powerful closing statement.

> There are helpful hints for children for writing a discursive text on page 135 of the Resource book.